Reader's Digest
Kitchen & Bathroom
DIY Manual

D1529836

Reader's Digest
Kitchen & Bathroom
DIY Manual

Expert guidance on renewing and renovating a kitchen or bathroom

Published by
The Reader's Digest Association Limited
London • New York • Sydney • Montreal

Contents

Introduction

6   Using this book

Understanding the systems

10   Mains water supply
12   Hot water supply
15   Waste water
16   Electrical system
18   Heating
20   Building and Wiring Regulations
22   Cutting off the power and water supply

Maintenance and repairs

26   Taps
32   Blocked sinks
34   WC problems
38   Showers
38   Replacing a pull-cord light switch

Fitting a new kitchen

Planning

42   Designing a layout
44   Choosing a style
48   Appliances, lighting and heat

Preparation

50   Planning the job
51   Removing old tiles and flooring
52   Repositioning services
54   Assembling flat-pack units

Installation

55 Installing units
57 Fitting cornice, pelmet and plinths
59 Fitting doors and handles
60 Cutting and fitting worktops
64 Plumbing the kitchen
72 Wiring in a cooker
76 Lighting

Fitting a new bathroom

Planning

82 Designing a layout
84 Choosing a style
87 Storage and lighting
90 Showers
94 Choosing taps

Installation

95 Planning the job
96 Replacing a bidet or washbasin
100 Replacing a bath
102 Replacing a WC
105 Installing a shower
106 Bathroom electrics

Finishing touches

112 Tiling
123 Painting

125 Index
128 Acknowledgments

Using this book

Whether you need to unblock the kitchen sink or fix a dripping bath tap, or are planning a major overhaul and refit of your kitchen or bathroom, this book has all the practical advice you need to keep everything in these two important rooms in good working order – and plenty of inspiration for creating stylish and functional new rooms, too.

BUILDING REGULATIONS

Many jobs that form part of major works in a kitchen or bathroom require Building Regulations approval from your local council Building Control Department.

All new wiring work in kitchens and bathrooms must be notified to your Building Control Department and, if you do the work yourself, checked and approved by a certified electrician, who is registered with the 'Competent Person Scheme'.

See pages 20–21 for more information. When you come to sell your home, you may be required to prove that any works that have been done comply with all the relevent regulations.

 All the wiring projects in this book that carry this symbol are notifiable.

---

difference to how you cut off the flow of water to make repairs or change a plumbing fitting. Chapter One explains how the systems work, how to identify what kind of set-up you have in your home and how to turn off the water and power so that you can work safely.

You'll also find a clear summary of what you need to know and do to conform with Building Regulations, and in particular the wiring restrictions that apply to kitchens and bathrooms. Make sure that you read this chapter before you do anything else.

Maintenance and repairs

Dripping taps, blocked sinks and a WC that won't flush are just some of the common faults and breakdowns that you might encounter. Chapter Two leads you through the maintenance and repairs you will need to keep your existing or newly fitted kitchen and bathroom in good working order.

They are two of the biggest DIY projects you are likely to tackle in the home: fitting a new kitchen and replacing a bathroom suite. They are also the two rooms where you most need to carry out regular maintenance to prevent problems from occuring. This book will lead you, step-by-step, through all the essential maintenance tasks and common repairs and give you clear and helpful advice on planning your use of space, scheduling a major refit and installing new fittings in accordance with the relevant Building Regulations.

Before you start

It is vital that you understand how your home's electric, plumbing and heating systems work before embarking on any repairs or home improvements – however small – in your kitchen and bathroom.

The kind of water supply system you have can affect your choice of taps and showers, for example, and will also make a

Fitting a new kitchen

Chapter Three tells you all you need to know to install a new kitchen. There is advice on planning your layout to make best use of the space you have available, stylish ideas for choosing cupboards and handles, clever storage solutions and helpful tips on choosing kitchen taps and appliances – and the waste pipes and traps that you will need.

Once you have ordered your units and appliances, you'll find a clear program for planning the works to minimise the disruption to your cooking facilities and advice on removing your old kitchen and re-routeing pipes and electrics if you are changing the layout.

Now you are ready to start installing the new units, follow the clear instructions for every step of the job, from assembling flat-pack carcasses to making professional joints in worktops, pelmets and cornice, hanging and adjusting cupboard doors and fitting an inset sink.

Here you will find step-by-step advice on joining water supply and waste pipes to take plumbing to taps and appliances, and away from the sink and washing machine, for example. The book also leads you through plumbing in a washing machine or dishwasher and wiring in an electric cooker. Finally, there is advice on fitting stylish low-voltage spotlights in your kitchen ceiling and wiring in under-cupboard lights to illuminate your worktops.

From start to finish, with the help of this book you can be sure of doing a professional job that you can be proud of.

Replacing your bathroom suite and fittings

If you are planning to renew your bathroom suite it is worth taking the opportunity to think about whether you are making the best use of your space. Bathrooms are often small and it is vital to plan carefully if you are to fit in all the different elements you want and make the room comfortable to use. Follow Chapter Four's useful guidelines about how much space to allow in front of a basin or around a WC or shower so that you won't be bumping your elbows when you dry yourself or squeezing past the toilet to get into the shower.

As with kitchens, bathrooms come in many different styles, from antique reproduction to cutting edge modernity. You'll find tips on all the different options and inspiration for creating ingenious storage solutions, choosing appropriate lighting and more.

The book will help you to plan the works efficiently to minimise disruption and gives you clear step-by-step instructions for every stage of the job, from replacing a basin, bath and WC to wiring in electrical appliances and shaver sockets.

Adding the finishing touches

Finally, Chapter Five will help you to finish the job with professional-looking tiling on splashbacks and around the bath and shower. And you'll find helpful decorating tips geared specifically towards painting in rooms that will often be hot and steamy.

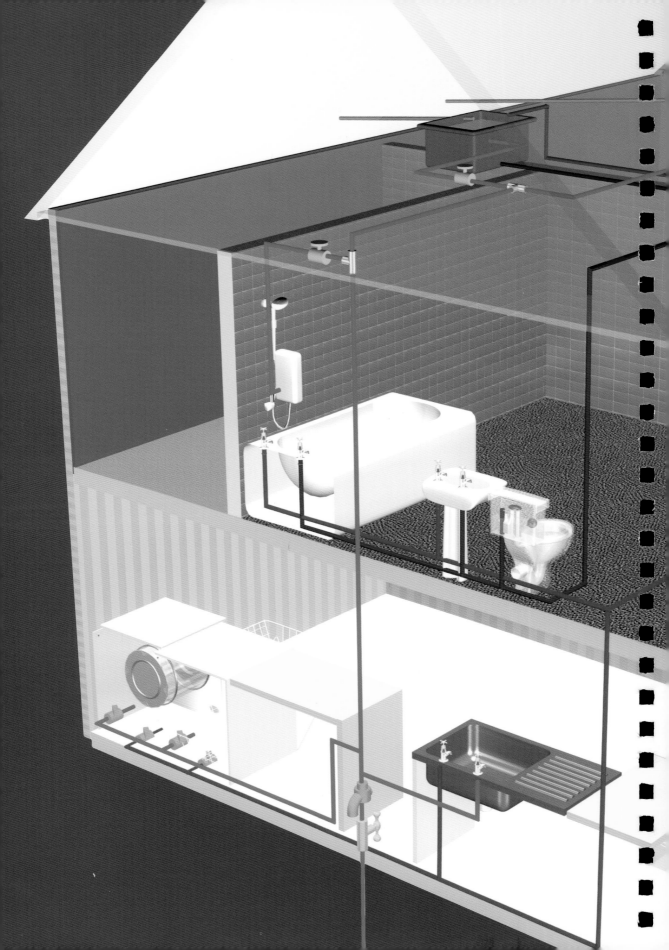

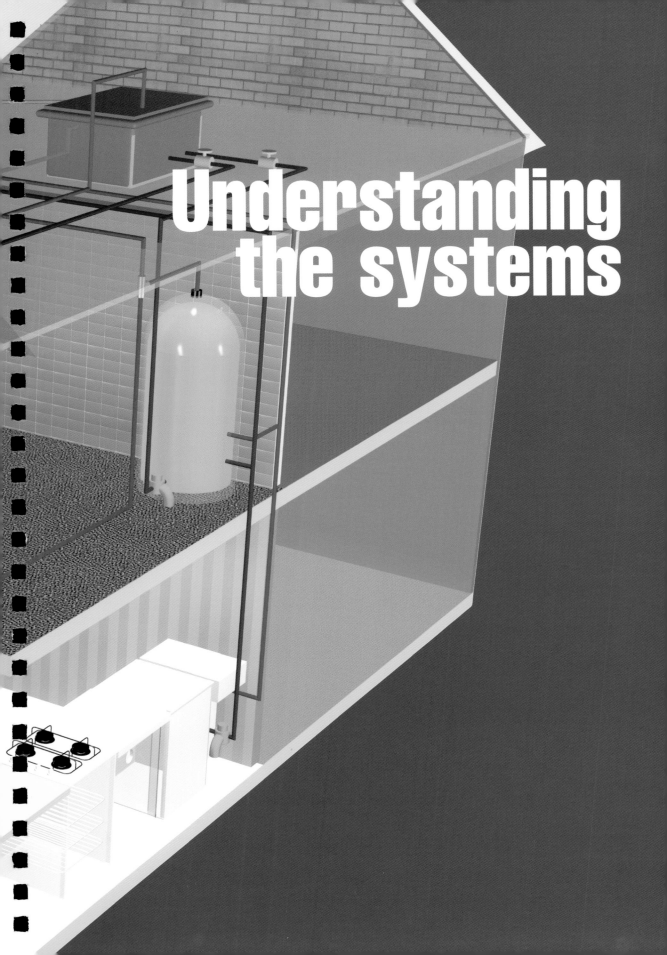

Understanding the systems

How water is supplied to the home

Whether for home improvements or for tackling emergencies, it is important to know what type of water system you have, and where to find all the relevant system controls.

The cold water supply

There are two types of cold water supply in British homes: direct and indirect.

In a direct cold water supply, branch pipes from the rising main lead directly to all the cold taps and WC cisterns in the house. This means that you can drink cold water from any tap. A pipe from the rising main will usually feed a storage cistern in the loft – the reservoir that feeds the hot water cylinder. A direct cold water system is simpler and cheaper to install than an indirect system.

Most British homes have an indirect system. The rising main feeds the cold tap at the kitchen sink (and possibly pipes to a washing machine and an outside tap). This water is clean drinking water. It then continues up to a cold water storage tank in the roof, which supplies all other taps, the WCs and the hot water cylinder.

Water meter If the property has a water meter, it will be installed outside the property boundary, between the mains and the outdoor stoptap.

Water mains The water supply to most British homes is provided by the local water supply company, through iron or heavy plastic water mains.

Communication pipe From the mains, a pipe known as a communication pipe takes the water to the water company's stoptap – a control valve about 1m below the ground at or near the boundary of each property.

Rising main The service pipe enters the house, usually close to the kitchen sink (but sometimes under the stairs or in a garage), and from there is known as the rising main. Another stoptap for cutting off the house water supply should be fitted where the pipe enters the house. The rising main is usually a 15mm diameter pipe, but in areas where mains pressure is low, a 22mm diameter pipe is used.

To cold water cistern (or direct draw-off points)

Rising main with indoor stoptap

Guard pipe

Water mains

Communication pipe

Outdoor stoptap

Service pipe

Outdoor stoptap The stoptap, which is turned with a long key, is at the bottom of an earthenware guard pipe under a small metal cover, set into the surface of the garden or the public footpath outside. In older properties, this may be the only place where the water can be turned off.

Service pipe From the water company's stoptap, a service pipe carries water into the house. To avoid frost damage, it should be at least 750mm and not more than 1.35m below ground.

There are advantages to an indirect system: water from a cold water storage cistern gives even water pressure, which produces quieter plumbing and less wear and tear on washers and valves. Leaks are also less likely, and any leak that does occur will be less damaging than one from a pipe under mains pressure.

Water from a cistern is warmer than mains water, so less hot water is needed for washing and bathing. It also reduces condensation on WC cisterns. And if the house supply is temporarily cut off – for work on the mains, for example – there is a supply of stored water available for use.

Water pressure

Pressure is the force that pushes water through pipes, determining the flow of water from the taps in your house. If the pressure is not high enough or the service pipe is too small, then the flow can be reduced and it will take a long time to fill a cistern or bath. If water pressure is too high it can wear down joints and piping in your system, causing leaking water heaters, banging pipes, dripping taps and more.

Water companies must provide water to a specific pressure at your stop tap (pressure is measured in bars: 1bar is the minimum required pressure). Water is usually provided at about 3bar and in some areas may be as high as 7bar. If your water pressure seems too high you can fit pressure reducing valves. If you think the pressure is too low, consult your water company.

Water softeners and purifiers

Mains water contains certain amounts of chlorine and various other dissolved minerals. There are also traces of metals, nitrates, insecticides and herbicides. The simplest way to remove contaminants from drinking water is the jug filter, which sits on the worktop and is filled by hand. Its activated carbon filter removes chlorine and pesticides and an ion-exchange system removes metals and reduces hardness.

Plumbed-in systems The most common plumbed-in system is attached to the incoming water supply so that water used for bathing and washing clothes is softened but drinking water remains untreated. This is especially important for babies and people on a sodium-restricted diet. The system works by passing the water through resin beads that replace the scale-forming magnesium and calcium ions with harmless and flavour-free sodium ions. The beads are regenerated by periodically flushing through with salt water to replenish the supply of sodium ions and remove the calcium and magnesium ions. The unit must be fitted near to the incoming service pipe, stop tap, and near to a drain for used salt water.

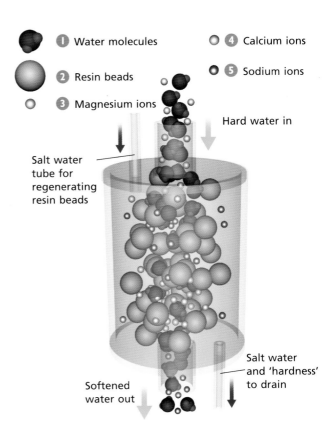

1 Water molecules
2 Resin beads
3 Magnesium ions
4 Calcium ions
5 Sodium ions

Hard water in

Salt water tube for regenerating resin beads

Softened water out

Salt water and 'hardness' to drain

Hot water supply

There are two basic hot water systems: either indirect, with all hot taps supplied from a hot water storage cylinder, or direct, where cold water is heated on demand. The latter is usual when all the cold water supplies come direct from the rising main.

Back boilers and separate kitchen boilers have largely been replaced by modern boilers that supply both hot water and central heating.

Instantaneous hot water systems
Single point water heaters may be heated by gas or electricity and are usually sited next to the point they serve. In the case of electric heaters, such as an electric shower, they must be wired to the mains via an isolating switch. Many homes are now being fitted with multipoint water heaters – most commonly combination (combi) boilers. A combi boiler combines the functions of a central heating boiler and an instantaneous multipoint water heater.

Indirect systems

You can identify an indirect system (see page 14) by the two water tanks in the loft. The second, smaller one, has a vent pipe over the top. This is called a header tank, or feed and expansion tank; it keeps the primary circuit topped up. The level of water in the header tank is low enough to allow the water to rise as it expands when it gets hot without overflowing.

The primary circuit With an indirect water system, the hot water cylinder contains a coil of pipe, which forms part of a run of pipework attached to the boiler. This is heated directly by the boiler. Indirectly, it heats the water in the cylinder. The coil, or heat exchanger, is actually part of the central heating circuit: its water heating function arises out of its main job, which is to heat the radiators. This heating pipework is known as the 'primary' circuit and the pipes that run to and from the boiler are known as the primary flow and return.

Primary circuit water constantly circulates while the boiler is on. The hot water tank itself works in the same way as one in a direct system.

The secondary circuit Water in the hot water cylinder is supplied from the cold water cistern, which keeps the cylinder constantly topped up as hot water is used. A vent pipe from the top of the hot water cylinder hangs over the cold water cistern, allowing air to escape. Pipes to the hot taps lead from the vent pipe. Because these branch pipes leave above the cylinder top, the cylinder cannot be drained through the hot taps. This means you don't need to turn off the boiler if the household water supply is temporarily cut off.

This system is known as a vented system. It is open to atmospheric pressure and operates under low pressure. A pump can be fitted to boost flow to showers or taps.

Unvented (sealed) hot water systems
This system is the same as an indirect system, except that it is connected to the mains. This gives mains water pressure to hot taps and showers. Many safety features are built into this type of system to allow for the greater pressure and expansion of the water. No cold water storage cistern or header tank is needed, so there is no pipework in the loft.

Direct systems

In older houses with a direct system (often back boilers or solid-fuel boilers), the water is heated directly by circulation through the boiler. Water is fed from the cold water cistern into the bottom of the cylinder and then to the boiler. The flow pipe from the top of the boiler discharges hot water directly into the top of the cylinder, forcing colder, denser water at the bottom through the return pipe back to the boiler. The hottest water, being the lightest, is always at the top ready to be drawn off.

Immersion heater This is another form of direct heating. The hot water cylinder can be heated by one or two electric immersion heaters. About 1kW of heat is needed for every 45 litres of water, so a 140-litre hot water cylinder needs a 3kW heater. Today, an immersion heater is rarely the sole form of water heating in the home. Rather, it is used to supplement a boiler system or as a way to heat water in summer when the central heating boiler is switched off.

An immersion heater has a thermostat to control the water temperature. For most homes, 55–60°C is ideal.

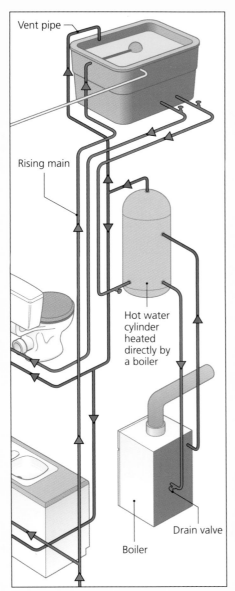

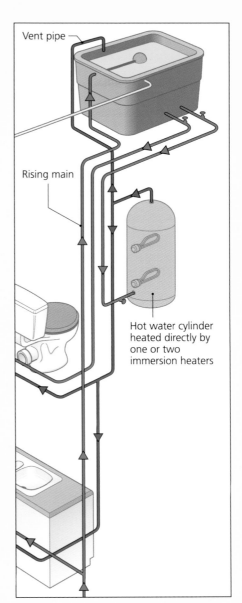

Direct heat Hot water in the cylinder is heated by circulation through the boiler. The system cannot be used to supply central heating radiators.

Immersion heater Hot water stored in the cylinder is heated directly by electric immersion heater. The system cannot be used to supply central heating radiators.

A typical indirect (two circuit) system

1 The rising main feeds the kitchen cold tap and kitchen appliances before it rises to the cold water storage cistern.

2 The cold water cistern is filled from the rising main, and the inflow of water is controlled by a float-operated ballvalve. The capacity of the average household cistern is 230 litres, and it has an overflow pipe to carry water out to the eaves if the cistern overfills through a failure of the ballvalve.

3 Water regulations require new cold water storage cisterns and header tanks (feed and expansion tanks) to have dust-proof and insect-proof (but not airtight) covers and to be insulated against frost. The storage cistern must supply drinkable water.

4 Water from the cistern is distributed by at least two 22mm (or 28mm) diameter pipes fitted about 75mm from the bottom. One supplies WCs and cold taps – except for the kitchen cold tap. Normally the 22mm pipe goes direct to the bath cold tap, and 15mm branches feed washbasins and WC cisterns.

5 The other distribution pipe feeds cold water to the bottom of the hot water cylinder – usually a copper cylinder of about 140 litres capacity. In a typical modern house with a central heating boiler, there are two water circuits through the hot water cylinder – the primary circuit that heats the water, and the secondary circuit that distributes it (see page 12).

6 Hot water stored in the cylinder is heated indirectly by the primary water circuit through the boiler, and sometimes by an immersion heater as well. This system can also heat radiators.

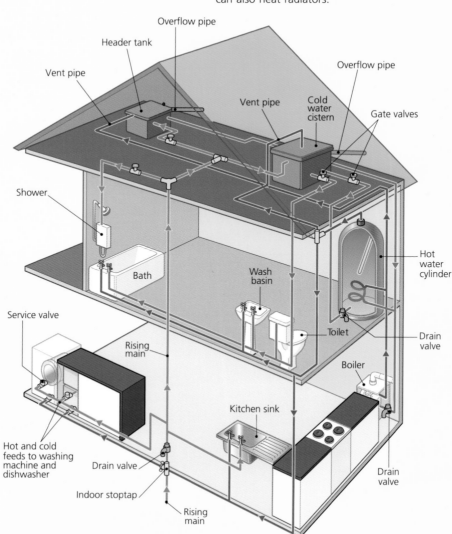

Overflow pipe
Header tank
Vent pipe
Overflow pipe
Vent pipe
Cold water cistern
Gate valves
Shower
Hot water cylinder
Bath
Wash basin
Toilet
Drain valve
Service valve
Boiler
Rising main
Kitchen sink
Hot and cold feeds to washing machine and dishwasher
Drain valve
Drain valve
Indoor stoptap
Rising main

Where the waste water goes

If you live in a house built before the mid-1960s, you probably have a two pipe drainage system; newer houses have one drain pipe – a single stack system.

Whatever the drainage system, every bath, basin or sink in the house is fitted with a trap – a bend in the outlet pipe below the plughole. This holds sufficient water to stop gases from the drains entering the house and causing an unpleasant smell. The trap has some means of access for clearing blockages. All WC pans have built-in traps.

Below ground, the household waste pipes or drains are channelled through an inspection chamber near the house to form the main drain, which runs into the water company's sewer.

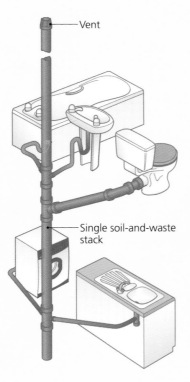

Vent

Single soil-and-waste stack

Single stack system

Modern houses have a single stack drainage system. Waste from all sinks and WCs is carried underground by a single vertical pipe known as a soil stack. This pipe may be installed inside the house and its vented top extends above the roof.

Two pipe system

Most houses built before the mid-1960s have what is known as a two pipe drainage system for waste water disposal.

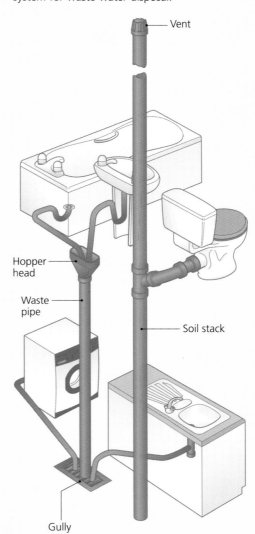

Vent

Hopper head

Waste pipe

Soil stack

Gully

• A vertical soil stack fixed to an outside wall carries waste from upstairs WCs to an underground drain.
• The open top of the soil stack – the vent – extends above the eaves and allows the escape of sewer gases. It is protected from birds with a metal or wire mesh guard.
• Ground floor WCs have an outlet direct into the underground drain.
• A second outside pipe – the waste pipe – takes used water from upstairs baths, basins and showers via an open hopper head to empty into a ground-level gully. Water from the kitchen sink also runs into a gully.

The electrical system

Before you do any electrical work you should get to grips with the different types of circuit in your home.

Electric power is measured in **watts** (W). The flow of electricity is called current, and is measured in **amps** (A). The driving force, or pressure, of the current is measured in **volts** (V). The pressure of public supply in Britain has been standardised at 230 volts. In Britain, mains electricity is **alternating current** (AC) and the electricity from batteries is **direct current** (DC). The advantage of alternating current is that it can be transformed from one voltage to another so a power station can supply a very high voltage to substations that reduce the voltage to 230V to supply homes.

Lighting circuit The circuit runs out from the consumer unit, linking a chain of lighting points. Cables run from each lighting point to its switch. The circuit is protected by a 5 or 6amp circuit fuse or MCB. It can safely supply up to a maximum of about 1200 watts, but in practice should not serve more than ten lighting points. The circuit would be overloaded if each of the lighting points had high-wattage bulbs.

Ring main circuit The circuit is wired as a ring that starts from the consumer unit and returns to it, allowing current to flow to socket outlets either way round the ring. It can serve a floor area of up to 100m². It is protected by a 30 or 32amp circuit fuse or MCB. It can have any number of sockets or fused connection units on it, but its maximum total load is about 7000 watts. For larger total loads and larger floor areas, additional ring circuits are needed.

Spur on a ring circuit Extra socket outlets can be added to an existing ring main circuit via spurs branching off the ring at a socket outlet or junction box. In theory, each outlet on the ring could supply a spur to a single or double socket or a fused connection unit. However, the circuit including any spurs must not serve rooms with a floor area of more than 100m² – and its maximum load is still 7000 watts.

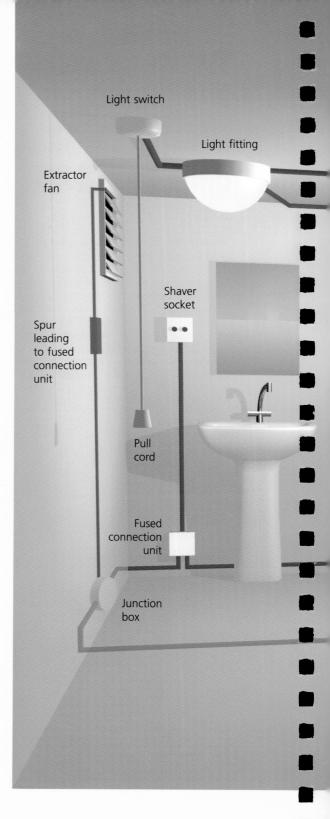

Light switch

Light fitting

Extractor fan

Shaver socket

Spur leading to fused connection unit

Pull cord

Fused connection unit

Junction box

Socket outlet The maximum load that can be supplied by a socket outlet taking a 13amp plug is 3000 watts. The plug is fitted with a 13amp or a 3amp fuse, according to the wattage rating of the appliance connected to it.

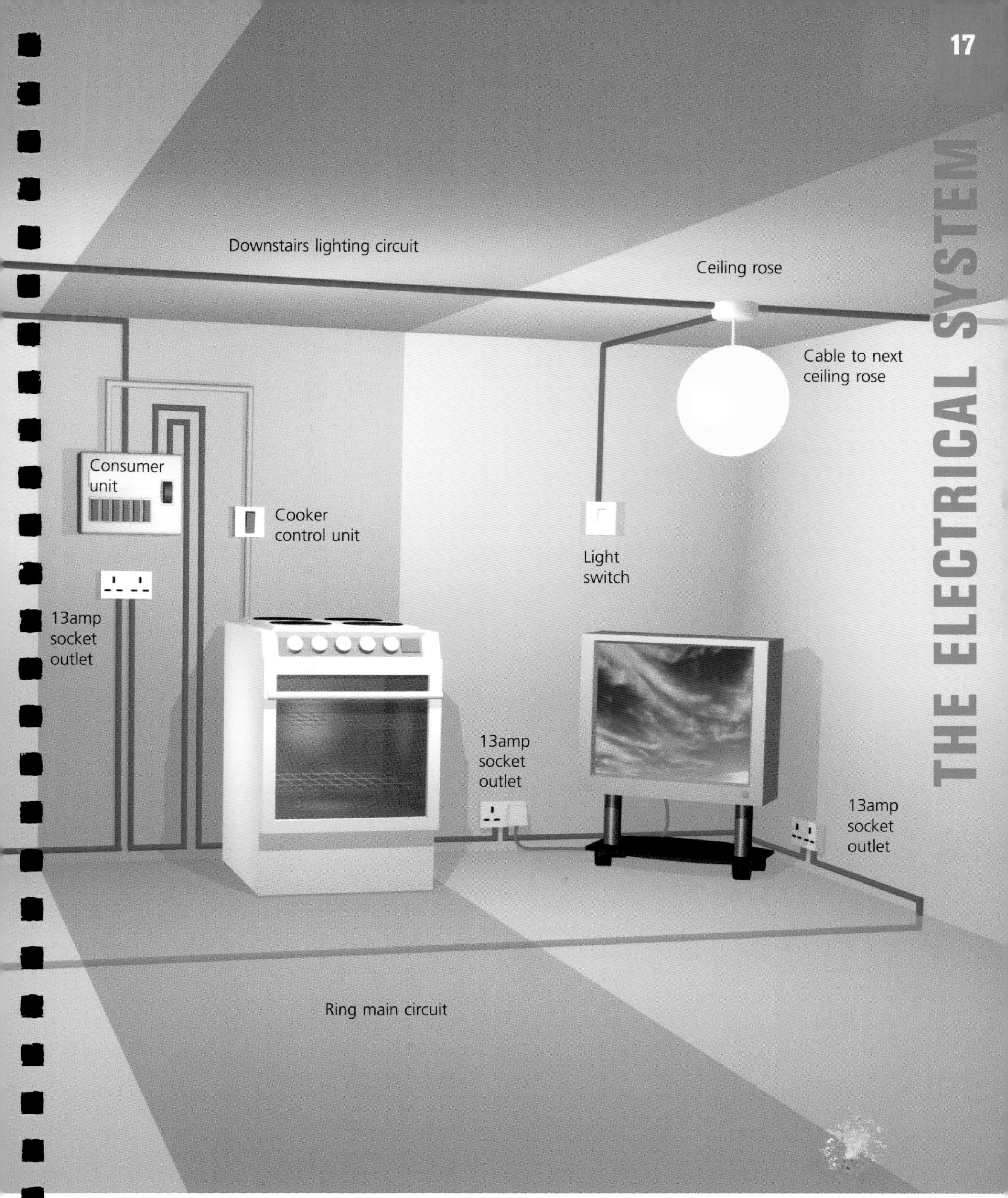

Downstairs lighting circuit

Ceiling rose

Cable to next
ceiling rose

Consumer
unit

Cooker
control unit

Light
switch

13amp
socket
outlet

13amp
socket
outlet

13amp
socket
outlet

Ring main circuit

Single-appliance circuit An appliance that is a large consumer of electricity and in constant or frequent use – a cooker, a fixed water heater, or a shower heater unit, for example – has its own circuit running from the consumer unit. It would take too large a proportion of the power available on a shared circuit and would be likely to cause an overload.

Heating options in kitchens and bathrooms

Kitchens and bathrooms can both be awkward rooms to heat. Follow this advice for making them comfortable rooms to use.

When you are cooking, the temperature in a kitchen can sometimes get uncomfortably high, yet many people use their kitchen as a busy family living area, so it is important that it should be warm on chilly days when the oven is not on. To help to keep the room at a comfortable and stable temperature it is important to fit thermostatic radiator valves (TRVs) to any radiators on the central heating system. These valves will close off the radiator when the room reaches your desired temperature, rather than the radiator and cooker both continuing to give out heat.

Radiator alternatives

In smaller kitchens it can be difficult to create space for a radiator. Wall space may be better used by extra cupboards. In these situations, an ingenious, space-saving option is a plinth heater that fits into the gap between the cupboard base and the floor. They can be simple electrical fan convector heaters, operated manually by a switch or may be linked to the rest of the central heating system. In this case, an electrical fan blows air across copper fins, which are heated by hot water from the central heating circuit when it is on. Low voltage versions are available for use in bathrooms. A filter in the air intake traps dirt and should be regularly cleaned to maintain maximum performance and to prevent noise.

In a bathroom it is possible to combine the radiator with a towel rail. Electric or centrally heated towel rails alone seldom produce enough heat to keep the room as warm as is necessary, but a radiator that has additional heated rails for hanging towels will do both jobs at once. You can also buy towel rail radiators with an additional electrical heating element to warm the rail when the heating is switched off (page 108).

Underfloor heating

This is a popular and effective heating option in both bathrooms and kitchens. It may not produce enough heat for the coldest of winters, but is an excellent solution for maintaining a comfortable ambient temperature.

Underfloor heating warms the entire surface of the floor. Even in a small room, this is a large radiant surface, which means that the heat running through the heating elements needs to be only slightly hotter than the room. By contrast, a radiator transfers heat from a very small surface, and has to be much hotter than the room it is heating. Typically, the temperature of the water in an underfloor heating system pipe is 45–65°C compared to the 80°C surface temperature of a radiator. Most

underfloor systems warm the floor to 25–28°C, which is comfortable to walk on. There are two main underfloor heating systems – water, which operates along with the central heating system, and electric, controlled by a dedicated thermostat and timer or programmer.

Underfloor heating: advantages
• Underfloor heating is unobtrusive, freeing up walls which might otherwise have radiators against them. In addition, it is quiet in use. There is even distribution of heat across each room, and individual room temperature control.
• It is safer than other systems of central heating: there is no risk of contact with surfaces that are too hot.
• The electric mat system is easy to install and requires no special skills.

Underfloor heating: disadvantages
• Heating systems cannot respond rapidly to quick temperature changes, and have longer heat-up and cooling-down periods than other forms of central heating.
• There is greater disruption when installing an underground heating system in an existing building than with other systems.
• The choice of floor finishing requires careful consideration, and changes of floor finish may affect performance. It is advisable to avoid solid wood or laminate floor finishes, that may be affected by the frequent temperature changes. Stone or ceramic tiles work well.

Water heated systems
Water systems use warm water pumped through small diameter (usually 10mm) plastic pipes which run up and down the sub-floor. The pipes are linked into the building's central heating system. They warm the floor, which in turn warms the room above. Pipes can be installed when the building is constructed or, in some cases, fitted later.

In a new construction (such as a conservatory extension) with a solid ground floor, pipes are laid within the sand-and-cement screed. Insulation beneath the pipework ensures that heat is directed into

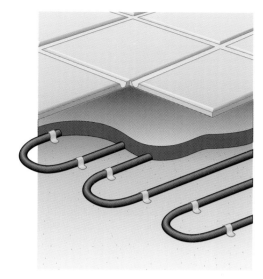

the room and energy is not wasted in heating the concrete foundations.

On upper floors and suspended wood floors (with joists and floorboards), heating pipes can be laid between the joists. An insulation layer underneath the pipework prevents the ceiling of the room below from getting warm and directs heat to where it is needed: the room above.

A water system is best installed by a qualified contractor.

Electric systems
An alternative to a wet system is an electric system. This is easier to fit, and is a more realistic DIY option. An electric mat, similar in appearance to an electric blanket, is laid on the floor, and your chosen floor covering laid on top.

Many companies supply their products to both the trade and DIY consumer, and most have technical departments that supply installation instructions and even check the completed system.

SAFETY TIP

Before working on electrical systems, isolate electrical circuits and check with a tester before touching any wires or cables. If you are in any doubt about what you are doing, seek specialist advice.

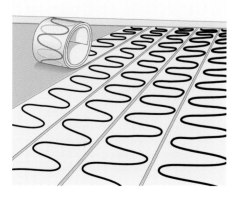

Building Regulations

It is important to be aware of your responsibility to conform with Building Regulations requirements when doing work on your home. Kitchens and bathrooms have rules specific to them.

Before you start work on a major refit of a kitchen or bathroom, contact your local Building Control Department to discuss the work you have planned. If the work involves alterations to or new connections into an existing drainage stack or underground drain, for example, you may need their approval. If you are just replacing fittings like-for-like then this can probably be done outside the scope of the Building Regulations.

All new domestic wiring work in England and Wales must comply with the requirements of a new section of the Building Regulations. Part P, entitled Electrical Safety, covers the design, installation, inspection and testing of electrical work in the home. It applies to both professional and DIY electrical work. Minor electrical work to movable appliances can be done without approval, but more major wiring jobs must be notified to the local Building Control Department.

Jobs that must be notified

Most wiring jobs carried out in kitchens and bathrooms must be notified to your local building control department before you start work. These include:

- **The installation of any new indoor circuit, such as one supplying an electric shower or a home extension.**
- **Any new wiring work in a kitchen or bathroom. This includes the addition to an existing circuit of new lighting points, socket outlets or fused spurs, the installation or upgrading of equipotential bonding, and the installation of electric under-floor heating. But replacement of existing equipment in either type of room is exempt from notification.**
- **The installation of extra-low-voltage lighting circuits. But the installation on existing lighting circuits of pre-assembled extra-low-voltage light fittings with CE approval is exempt.**

WIRING REGULATIONS

All projects in this book that carry this symbol are notifiable.

The local authority will inspect your work for a fee of around £100-£200. If you are in any doubt as to whether the work you plan to do requires notification, contact your local authority building control department for advice.

Getting approval

DIY wiring work is still permitted following the introduction of Part P, but completed work must be inspected and tested by a 'competent person' to ensure that it complies with the new regulations. Depending on the scale of the work involved, you may also have to notify your local authority Building Control Department (see left). In this case, you must pay a Building Control fee to have the work inspected and tested and the relevant certificates issued on completion.

Employing an electrician

You may decide to employ a professional to carry out wiring work for you. It is recommended that you use an electrician who is registered with the 'Competent Person Scheme'. For minor electrical work, a registered electrician will issue a *Minor Electrical Installation Works Certificate* when the job has been completed. For major work, a registered electrician is not required to notify the local authority. When the work is completed you will receive a *Building Regulations Self-certification Certificate* and an *Electrical Installation Certificate*. You can use an electrician who is not registered with the 'Competent Person Scheme' but they must be qualified and registered with a recognised trade body such as NICEIC. He or she can issue you with the same certificates but must notify the local authority before carrying out any major electrical work.

New cable core colours

Since 1 April 2006, any new cable installed may have different core colours from your existing wiring, as part of a process of harmonisation across the EU. Illustrations and instructions in this book use the new colours where new cable is being installed.

Wiring in bathrooms

The Wiring Regulations define areas (called zones) in bathrooms where specific safety rules must be followed.

These describe what electrical equipment can be installed in each zone, and also how cables to that equipment must be routed.

Bathroom switches

All switches in the bathroom must be outside the zones, except for any switches that are an integral part of an appliance suitable for use within that particular zone. Pull-cord ceiling switches can be installed if the ceiling exceeds 2.25m in height, so long as they are outside zone 2 beside the bath or shower. If the ceiling is less than 2.25m high, all light and appliance switches must be outside the room.

Bathroom zones

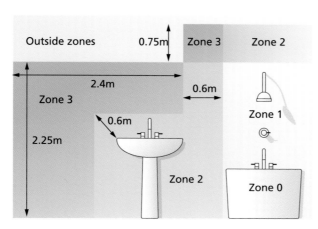

Zone 0 is the inside of the bath or shower tray. No electrical equipment is permitted here. The space beneath the bath is outside any zone if the bath panel is secured with screws and cannot be removed without the use of a screwdriver. This makes it suitable for the installation of equipment such as a shower pump. If there is no panel, or if the panel can be removed without tools, the area beneath the bath is zone 1.

Zone 1 is the space immediately above the bath or shower tray, and extends to a height of 2.25m above the floor. Within this zone you can install an instantaneous shower or water heater or an all-in-one power shower unit with a waterproof integral pump and their wiring.

CHOOSING LIGHTS FOR A BATHROOM

Strict regulations govern the use of electric light fittings in wet areas. When choosing lights for a bathroom, think about the position of the fitting and choose a light with an IP rating (indicating how waterproof it is) suitable for the appropriate zone. If water jets are likely to be used for cleaning purposes in any of these zones, a fitting rated to a minimum of IP65 must be used.

Zone 1	IP44, protected by an RCD if mains voltage (240V)
Zone 2	IP44
Zone 3	No IP rating required

Zone 2 extends horizontally to 600mm from the edge of zone 1, and vertically to a height of 2.25m above floor level. It also extends to 600mm all round a basin, bidet or WC. If the ceiling of the room is higher than 2.25m, the area above zone 1 is also designated as zone 2 up to a height of 3m. Within zone 2 you can install: any of the equipment allowed in zone 1; light fittings (see the box below left); a shaver unit that complies with British Standard BS EN 60742; an extractor fan; a whirlpool unit connected to the bath; the wiring to these appliances and any in zone 1.

Zone 3 extends horizontally for 2.4m beyond zone 2, and vertically to a height of 2.25m above the floor. In addition, the area above zone 2 next to the bath or shower is also designated as zone 3, up to a height of 3m. Within zone 3 you can install: any equipment allowed in zones 1 and 2; any fixed appliance such as a room heater or towel rail, so long as it is protected by a 30 milliamp residual current device (RCD); and the relevant wiring.

Cable routes

The cable to any appliance must be routed either within its zone, or through an adjacent zone designated with a higher number. You may not run cables to an appliance in one zone through a zone with a lower number, even if they are buried in the wall plaster.

Turning off the power

It is essential to isolate any electrical appliances and circuits before you attempt any work on them. Follow these safety precautions to avoid risk of injury, but if you are in any doubt about your ability to complete a job, always seek professional help.

Isolate mains circuits at the consumer unit (below) by switching off the appropriate miniature circuit breakers (MCBs) or removing the circuit fuses. If you have an electric cooker, it should be on a dedicated 30amp circuit, separate from the other electrical appliances. A freezer is also often run on its own circuit to reduce the risk of it being switched off and defrosting when another appliance or fault trips a circuit elsewhere in the house.

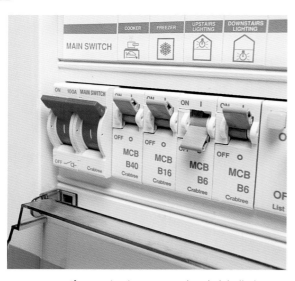

If your circuits are not already labelled at the consumer unit, it is a good idea to do this. To identify the circuits, turn off the main switch and switch off one MCB at a time. Turn the main switch back on and check which lights or appliances are not working.

Isolate any appliance that is wired into a fixed flex-outlet plate in bathrooms and kitchens by switching off the fused connection unit (FCU) that supplies it. Most FCUs have a neon light to indicate whether the power is on or off.

Cutting off the water supply

Before you start work on any plumbing jobs in the kitchen or bathroom you will need to turn off the water supply.

If you are plumbing in new fittings in the same place as the old ones, cutting off the water supply may be a simple job. Modern houses and those that have had plumbing fittings replaced in recent years may already have isolator or service valves fitted in the pipe run to each tap or WC. If this is the case, you need only turn the screw on the valve to the closed position and drain off the small amount of water left in the pipe.

A GOOD TIME TO ADD SERVICE VALVES

Draining down the system for repairs or replacement presents an excellent opportunity to fit service valves on the pipes supplying every tap and WC cistern ballvalve. Having done this, you will be able to repair or replace any tap or ballvalve without having to drain the system beforehand.

If you do not have isolator valves fitted, you will need to turn off the water to part of the house or to the whole house from the main stoptap. In many homes, only the kitchen tap is fed from the rising main; others are fed from the cold water cistern. It depends whether the plumbing system is direct or indirect (page 10).

Taps fed from the cistern

1 To isolate a hot or cold tap supplied from the cistern, turn off the gatevalve on the supply pipe from the cistern. If a service valve (see page 30) is fitted in the pipe to the tap, turn it off with a screwdriver.

2 Turn on the tap until the water has stopped flowing.

Alternatively If there is no gatevalve or service valve on the pipe, you will have to drain the cistern.

Draining the cistern

1 Tie the ballvalve arm to a piece of wood laid across the cistern (see page 31). This stops the flow from the mains.

2 Turn on the bathroom cold taps until the water stops flowing, then turn on the hot taps – very little water will flow from them. (You need not turn off the boiler, as the hot water cylinder will not be drained.)

HELPFUL TIP

A stoptap that has been open for a long time may be jammed. To guard against this, close and open the stoptap fully twice a year. After opening it, give the handle a quarter turn towards closure. This prevents jamming without affecting water flow. If a stoptap is difficult to turn, apply a few drops of penetrating oil round the spindle base and leave for ten minutes before turning the handle again. Repeat as necessary.

TYPES OF STOPTAP AND ISOLATING VALVE

Stoptap A tap with a valve and washer that is inserted into a mains-pressure supply pipe to control the water flow through it. A stoptap is usually kept turned on, being turned off only when necessary to cut off the supply. It must be fitted the right way round (an arrow mark shows the flow direction). Most stoptaps have a crutch handle.

Drain valve A tap without a handle, opened by turning the spindle with a drain valve key. It is normally kept closed, but has a ribbed outlet for attaching a hose when draining is necessary. A drain valve is fitted in those parts of the plumbing system that cannot be drained through household taps – for instance, in the boiler or central-heating systems and on the rising main.

Gatevalve An isolating valve with a wheel handle, through which the water flow is controlled by raising or lowering a metal plate (or gate). It can be fitted either way round and is normally used in low-pressure pipes such as supply pipes from a storage cistern. With the gate open, the flow is completely unrestricted. When it is closed, the seal is not as watertight as a stoptap.

Service valve A small isolating valve operated with a screwdriver. This turns a pierced plug inside the valve to stop or restore the water flow. Normally used in a low-pressure supply pipe to a tap or ballvalve to cut off the water for repairs. A similar valve with a small lever handle and a threaded outlet is used to control the flow to the flexible supply hoses of a washing machine or dishwasher.

CUTTING OFF POWER & WATER

Maintenance and repairs

How taps work

All taps work in much the same way – a rotating handle opens and closes a valve inside the body of the tap. Traditional taps, such as the rising spindle, use a system of nuts and screws to open the valve; modern taps use rotating ceramic discs instead.

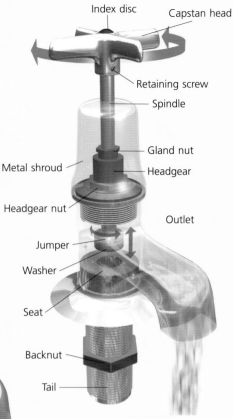

Index disc — Capstan head

Retaining screw

Spindle

Gland nut

Metal shroud

Headgear

Headgear nut

Outlet

Jumper

Washer

Seat

Backnut

Tail

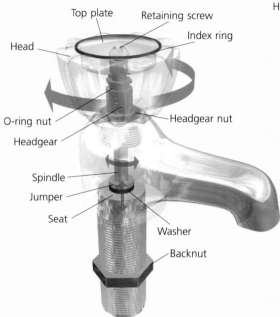

Top plate — Retaining screw

Index ring

Head

O-ring nut — Headgear nut

Headgear

Spindle

Jumper

Seat

Washer

Backnut

Non-rising spindle The jumper valve and washer are the same as in a traditional rising spindle tap, but the spindle is sealed by an O-ring nut rather than a gland nut. The tap handle and headgear have to be removed to change a washer or to renew an O-ring.

Rising spindle The jumper valve is in the shape of a rod and plate, and the washer is attached to the base of the plate. When changing a washer, the handle is lifted off with the headgear. When adjusting the gland nut, the handle has to be removed so that the bell-shaped cover can be pulled off out of the way.

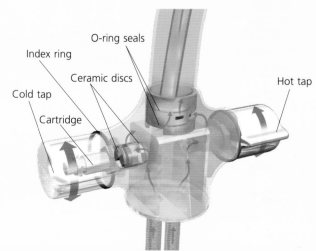

O-ring seals

Index ring

Ceramic discs

Cold tap

Hot tap

Cartridge

Ceramic disc tap In this type of tap, one ceramic disc is rotated against another until openings in the discs line up and water can flow through.

Repairing a dripping tap

A dripping tap usually means that the tap washer needs renewing, but can also be caused by a damaged valve seating. If the drip is from a mixer spout, renew both tap washers.

Tools *One large open-ended spanner, normally 20mm for a 12mm tap or 24mm for a 19mm tap (or use an adjustable spanner); old screwdriver (for prising). Possibly also one small spanner (normally 8mm); one or two pipe wrenches; cloth for padding jaws; one 5mm, one 10mm screwdriver.*

Materials *Replacement washer or a washer-and-jumper valve unit; alternatively, a washer-and-seating set; petroleum jelly. Possibly also penetrating oil.*

Removing the headgear

1 Cut off the water supply (page 23). Make sure the tap is turned fully on, and put the plug into the plughole to stop any small parts falling down the waste pipe.

2 Unscrew or lever off the cover of a non-rising spindle tap to expose the retaining screw. Remove the screw and put it in a safe place. Remove the head.

Alternatively With a rising spindle tap, prise off the index disc and remove the retaining screw to release the capstan from the spindle. Use a wrench wrapped in cloth to unscrew the metal shroud and lift it away from the headgear nut.

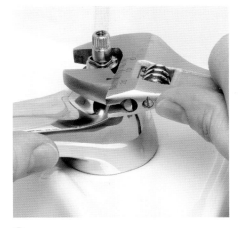

3 Undo the headgear nut with a spanner. Do not force the nut. If it is stiff, brace the tap body by hand or with a pipe wrench wrapped in a cloth, to prevent the tap from turning and fracturing the pipework attached to it.

4 If the nut is still difficult to turn, apply penetrating oil round the joint, wait about ten minutes to give it time to soak in, then try again. You may have to make several applications.

Fitting the washer

1 Prise off the washer with a screwdriver. If there is a small nut holding it in place, unscrew it with a spanner (normally 8mm). If it is difficult to undo, put penetrating oil round it and try again when it has soaked in. Then prise off the washer.

Alternatively If the nut is impossible to remove, you can replace both the jumper valve and washer in one unit.

2 After fitting a new washer or washer and jumper, grease the threads on the base of the tap before reassembling.

Repairing the valve seating

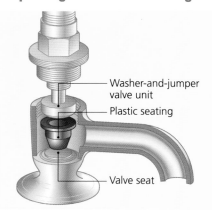

Washer-and-jumper valve unit

Plastic seating

Valve seat

When renewing a washer, inspect the valve seat inside the tap body. If it is scaled or scored by grit, the seal between washer and seat will not be effective even with a new washer.

The simplest repair is with a washer-and-seating set. This has a plastic seat to fit into the valve seat, and a washer-and-jumper valve unit to fit into the headgear.

When the tap is turned off, the plastic seating is forced firmly into place. It may take a few days for the new seating to give a completely watertight fit.

An alternative repair is to buy or hire a tap reseating tool and grind the seat smooth yourself.

AVOIDING HARD-WATER DAMAGE TO TAPS

If you live in a hard-water area, check your taps for damage, once a year.

Turn off the mains water supply. One at a time check that the headgear on each tap unscrews easily. Use penetrating oil to release stiff nuts and use a spanner and a wrench wrapped in a cloth to hold the body of the tap as you turn.

If limescale has built up, remove and soak small parts in vinegar or limescale remover. Smear the thread with lubricant before reassembling.

Tap conversion kits

You may be able to get tap conversion kits to change the style of taps and replace worn or broken mechanisms. Newer heads can be changed back to Victorian brass heads, or a tap with a crutch or capstan handle can be given a newer look. The spout and body of the tap remain in place.

Some kits have bushes to fit different tap sizes. The kits are available from most DIY stores and fitting instructions are included.

Cleaning or replacing ceramic discs

Ceramic disc taps operate on a different principle from conventional taps that have washers and spindles. Positioned in the body of the tap is a cartridge containing a pair of ceramic discs, each with two holes in it.

One disc is fixed in position; the other rotates when the handle is turned. As the movable disc rotates, the holes in it line up with the holes in the fixed one and water flows through them. When the tap is turned off the movable disc rotates so that the holes no longer align.

Dealing with a dripping tap

If a scratched ceramic disc is causing the leak, the entire cartridge must be replaced: left-handed for a hot tap or right-handed for a cold tap. Remove the old cartridge and take it with you when buying a replacement to make sure it is the correct size and 'hand'. Ceramic taps can also drip at the base of the cartridge if the seal has perished. Replace it if necessary.

Checking discs in a ceramic disc mixer tap

1 Turn off the water supply. Pull off the tap handles (it may be necessary to unscrew a small retaining screw on each) and use a spanner to unscrew the headgear section.

2 Carefully remove the ceramic cartridges, keeping hot and cold separate. Check both cartridges for dirt and wear and tear.

3 If the cartridges are worn, replace with identical parts for the tap unit. Make sure the hot and cold cartridges are fitted into the correct taps.

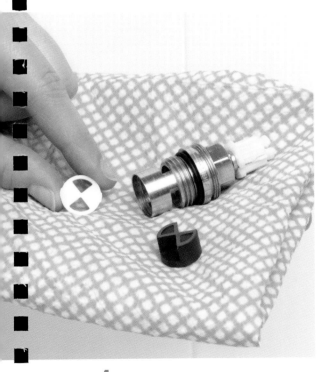

4 If the cartridges are dirty, clean them with a damp cloth. Replace the rubber seal, if it is worn. Replace the cartridge in the tap unit, fitting the hot and cold cartridges into the appropriate taps.

Curing a leak from a spindle or spout

Leakage from the body of the tap – from round the spindle, the base of a swivel spout, or the diverter knob on a shower mixer tap – may indicate a faulty gland or O-ring seal.

Possible causes This sort of leak is most likely to occur on a kitchen cold tap with a bell-shaped cover and visible spindle. Soapy water from wet hands may have run down the spindle and washed the grease out of the gland that makes a watertight joint round the spindle. If the tap is used with a garden hose, back pressure from the hose connection will also weaken the gland.

On a modern tap, especially one with a shrouded head, there is an O-ring seal instead of a gland, and it rarely needs replacing. However, an O-ring seal may occasionally become worn.

Tools *Small spanner (normally 12mm) or adjustable spanner. Possibly also one 5mm and one 10mm screwdriver; penknife or screwdriver for prising; two small wooden blocks about 10mm deep (such as spring clothes pegs).*

Materials *Packing materials (gland-packing string or PTFE tape). Possibly also silicone grease; O-rings (and possibly washers) of the correct size – take the old ones with you when buying, or give the make of tap.*

RELEASING THE SPINDLE

A non-rising spindle tap may have a circlip keeping the spindle in place. When you have removed the headgear, lever out the circlip so that you can gain access to the worn O-rings.

Adjusting the gland

There is no need to cut off the water supply to the tap.

1 With the tap turned off, undo the small screw that secures the capstan handle and put it in a safe place (it is very easily lost), then remove the handle. If there is no screw, the handle should pull off.

2 Remove the bell-shaped cover to reveal the gland nut – the highest nut on the spindle. Tighten the nut about half a turn with a spanner.

3 Turn the tap on by temporarily slipping the handle back on, then check whether there is still a leak from the spindle. If there is not, turn the gland nut another quarter turn and reassemble the tap. Do not overtighten the gland nut, or the tap will be hard to turn off.

4 If there is still a leak, give another half turn and check again.

5 If the gland continues leaking after you have adjusted it as far as possible, repack the gland.

Replacing the packing

1 With the tap turned off and the handle and cover removed, use a spanner to remove the gland nut and lift it out.

2 Pick out the old packing with a small screwdriver. Replace it with packing string from a plumbers' merchant or with PTFE tape pulled into a thin string. Pack it in with a screwdriver, then replace the gland nut and reassemble the tap.

Renewing the O-ring on a shrouded-head tap

1 Cut off the water supply to the tap (page 23) and remove the tap handle and headgear in the same way as for renewing a washer.

2 Hold the headgear between your fingers and turn the spindle clockwise to unscrew and remove the washer unit.

3 Prise out the O-ring at the top of the washer unit with a screwdriver or penknife.

4 Smear the new O-ring with silicone grease, fit it in position, and reassemble the tap.

Renewing O-rings on a kitchen mixer tap

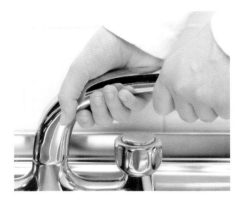

1 With both taps turned off, remove any retaining screw found behind the spout. If there is no screw, turn the spout to line up with the tap body and pull upwards sharply.

2 Note the position of the O-rings (probably two) and remove them.

3 Coat new O-rings of the correct size with silicone grease and fit them in position.

4 Smear the inside of the spout end with petroleum jelly, then refit it to the tap body.

Replacing shower-diverter O-rings

Diverters vary in design, but most have a sprung rod and plate attached to the diverter knob. When the knob is lifted, the plate opens the shower outlet and seals the tap outlet for as long as the shower is on.

1 With the bath taps turned off, lift the shower-diverter knob and undo the headgear nut with a spanner (probably 12mm size or use an adjustable spanner).

2 Lift out the diverter body and note the position of the washers and O-rings.

3 Remove the knob from the diverter body by turning it counter-clockwise. You may need to grip it with a wrench.

4 Withdraw the rod and plate from the diverter body and remove the small O-ring at the top of the rod.

5 Grease a new O-ring of the correct size with silicone grease and fit it in place.

6 Replace all other rubber washers and O-rings on the base of the rod and plate. Old ones may have to be prised out.

Dealing with an airlock

If the water flow from a tap (usually a hot tap) is poor when fully turned on, then hisses and bubbles and stops altogether, there is an airlock in the supply pipe.

Tools *Length of hose with a push-fit tap adaptor at each end. Possibly also dishcloth; screwdriver.*

1 Connect one end of the hose to the tap giving the trouble. If it is a bath tap and the hose is difficult to fit, connect to the nearby washbasin hot tap instead.

2 Connect the other end of the hose to the kitchen cold tap or to another mains-fed tap. Turn on the faulty tap first, then the mains-fed tap. The pressure of the mains water should blow the air bubble out of the pipe.

Important When applying mains pressure to a pipe in a stored-water circuit, there is a very slight risk of water from the system contaminating the mains water supply. Therefore you should do the job quickly and disconnect the hose immediately afterwards.

Airlock in a kitchen mixer

If the hot tap will not work, remove the swivel spout (page 31) and hold a cloth firmly over the spout hole while you turn on first the hot tap then the cold tap.

If airlocks keep occurring

There are many ways that air can be drawn into the water system and cause airlocks. Check these possibilities:

• Is the cold water cistern too small for the household's needs? If it is smaller than the standard 230 litres, replace it with one of standard size.

• Is the ballvalve in the cold water cistern sluggish? Watch the cistern emptying while the bath fills. If the valve does not open wide enough as water is drawn off, there will be a slow inflow and the cistern will empty before the bath is filled, allowing air to be drawn into the supply pipe. You may need to dismantle and clean the ballvalve.

• Is the supply pipe from the cold water cistern to the hot water cylinder obstructed or too narrow? Check that any gatevalve is fully open, and replace the pipe if it is narrower than 22mm in diameter. If hot water drawn for a bath is not replaced quickly enough, the water level in the vent pipe will fall below the level of the hot water supply pipe, and air will enter.

Dealing with a blocked sink

Grease may have built up in the trap and waste pipe, trapping food particles and other debris, or an object may be obstructing the waste pipe.

Tools *Possibly a length of wire; sink-waste plunger; sink auger or a length of expanding curtain wire; bucket.*

Materials *Caustic soda or proprietary chemical or enzyme cleaner; petroleum jelly.*

Sink slow to empty

If a sink is slow to empty, smear petroleum jelly on the rim of the plug hole to protect it, and then apply proprietary chemical or enzyme cleaner according to the manufacturer's instructions.

Sink completely blocked

1 If the water will not run away at all, place the sink plunger cup squarely over the plug hole.

2 Stuff a damp cloth firmly into the overflow opening and hold it there. This stops air escaping through the hole and dissipating the force you build up by plunging. Pump the plunger sharply up and down. If the blockage does not clear, repeat the operation.

3 If plunging fails, replace the sink plug. Put a bucket under the sink and disconnect the trap. Wash it out thoroughly if it is blocked with debris.

4 If the obstruction is not in the trap, try using a plumber's snake. It is a spiral device that can be hired or bought. Disconnect the blocked pipe from its trap and feed the wire into it. Then turn the handle to rotate the spiral. This drives its cutting head into the blockage and breaks it up.

Alternatively If you have a vacuum cleaner that is designed to cope with liquids, you can use it to try to dislodge a blockage in a sink trap. Press a cloth over the overflow in the sink. Then place the suction tube of the vacuum over the plughole and switch on. This will probably loosen the blockage sufficiently to allow it to be carried away by the water flow through the trap.

Alternatively If you have poured fat into the sink and it has hardened, try warming the pipe with a hair dryer, to melt the grease. Flush plenty of hot water after it.

Other pipe blockages

Washing machines and dishwashers are often plumbed in to feed the under-sink waste trap. Alternatively, they may join the main waste pipe at a T-junction away from the sink. If all your appliances feed into the one trap, you may need to disconnect all the pipes in turn and then clean each one to clear a blockage.

Repairing a faulty WC cistern

An overflow or a failure of a WC to flush properly are often caused by a faulty ballvalve, which governs the water level in the cistern.

Before you start Failure to flush properly is caused by either a low water level, or a worn or damaged flap valve. To determine the cause, first check the water level.

The plastic lever arm linking the spindle of the flush control to the siphon lift rod may eventually wear out and break. Replacement lever arms can be bought and are easily fitted.

Checking the water level

1 Remove the cistern lid (it may lift off or be held by one or more screws). When the cistern is full, the water level should be about 25mm below the overflow outlet. Or there may be a water level marked on the inside wall of the cistern.

2 If the level is low, repair or adjust the ballvalve by bending the arm up slightly or, with a modern diaphragm valve, loosening the locking nut and turning the adjuster to move it away from the plunger (see right).

If the level is too high and the cistern is overflowing or in danger of doing so, flush it, then repair or adjust the ballvalve.

If the level is correct, the problem is probably with the flap valve and you will need to renew it.

Adjusting the cistern water level

The normal level of a full cistern is about 25mm below the overflow outlet. The level can be raised by raising the float, or lowered by lowering the float.

Adjusting a ballvalve

Before you start If the cistern overflows, the water level is too high because the float either needs adjusting or is leaking and failing to rise to close the valve (or the valve itself may be faulty, right).

Tools *Possibly small spanner; vice.*

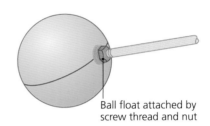

Ball float attached by screw thread and nut

On a **Portsmouth-pattern valve** with a ball float, unscrew and remove the float from the arm. To lower the level, hold the arm firmly in both hands and bend it slightly downwards. Then refit the float. If the arm is too stiff to bend in position, remove it from the cistern and grip it in a vice.

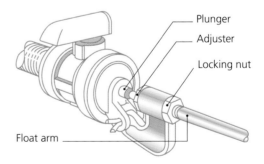

Plunger
Adjuster
Locking nut
Float arm

On a **diaphragm valve** with an adjuster at the top of the float arm, adjust the level by loosening the locking nut and screwing the adjuster forward, nearer to the plunger.

Alternatively Use an adjuster nut or clip near the float to move the float farther away from the valve along a horizontal arm, or to a lower position if it is linked to the arm by a vertical rod.

Renewing the flap valve in a standard siphon

A standard low-level suite has a full-sized cistern separate from the pan. The flap valve may be sold under the names siphon washer or cistern diaphragm. If you do not know the size you want, buy the largest available and cut it down.

A slimline cistern is repaired in the same way as a standard cistern, but some types are linked to the flush pipe with a locking ring-seal joint rather than with two nuts.

Tools *Screwdriver; wooden batten slightly longer than the cistern width; string; pipe wrench with a jaw opening of about 65mm; bowl or bucket. Possibly also sharp coloured pencil; scissors; container for bailing, or tube for siphoning.*

Materials *Plastic flap valve. Possibly also O-ring for ring-seal joint.*

1 With the cistern lid removed, lay a batten across the cistern and tie the float arm to it to stop the inflow of water.

2 Empty the cistern. If it cannot be flushed at all, bail or siphon the water out.

3 Use a large pipe wrench to undo the lower of the two large nuts underneath the cistern, then disconnect the flush pipe and push it to one side.

4 Put a bowl or bucket underneath the cistern and undo the large nut immediately under the cistern (this is the siphon-retaining nut). A pint or two of water will flow out as you loosen the nut.

5 Unhook the lift rod from the flushing lever, lift the inverted U-pipe (the siphon) out from the cistern and lay it on its side.

6 Pull out the lift rod and plate and remove the worn flap valve. If the new valve is too big, cut it down with scissors using the old valve as a pattern. It should touch, but not drag on, the dome sides.

7 Fit the new valve over the lift rod and onto the plate, then reassemble the flushing mechanism and reconnect the cistern.

Renewing the flap valve on a close-coupled suite

On some close-coupled suites, the siphon is held by two or more bolts inside the cistern rather than by a large nut underneath. Except for this difference, the flap valve is renewed in the same way as on a standard suite.

On others, the cistern must be lifted off in order to disconnect the siphon. The flap valve can then be renewed in the same way as on a standard suite. Lift off the cistern as follows:

1 Cut off the water supply to the cistern in the same way as for a tap (page 23). Empty the cistern by flushing, bailing or siphoning out the water.

2 Disconnect the overflow pipe and water supply pipe from the cistern. They generally have screw fittings with a back nut.

3 Undo the screws holding the cistern to the wall, and the wing nuts securing it to the rear platform of the pan.

4 Lift off the cistern from the pan and unhook the lift rod. Turn the cistern over, unscrew the retaining nut, remove the siphon and plate and renew the valve as above.

Renewing the flap valve on a two-part siphon

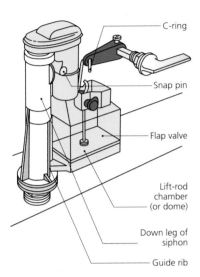

- C-ring
- Snap pin
- Flap valve
- Lift-rod chamber (or dome)
- Down leg of siphon
- Guide rib

If a cistern is fitted with a two-part plastic siphon, there is no need to stop the inflow or, with a close-coupled suite, to remove the cistern.

A two-part siphon can be fitted to most types of WC cistern. The initial fitting does involve cutting off the water supply and, if necessary, lifting off the cistern (see page 35). After that, maintenance is as below.

Tools *Screwdriver.*

Materials *Spares pack for size of siphon (containing flap valve); washers. Possibly also O-ring-seal.*

1 With the cistern lid removed, unhook the flush lever from the lift-rod C-ring. Remove a lever-type flush handle, as it may be in the way later.

2 Withdraw the snap pin about 30mm to disconnect the lift-rod chamber from the down leg of the siphon.

3 Slide the chamber upwards to disengage it from the guide rib on the down leg.

4 Remove the C-ring and washer from the top of the lift rod and slide the lift rod from the bottom of the chamber.

5 Take off the lift-rod washers and weight so that you can remove the old flap valve and fit a new one.

6 Before reassembling, check if the O-ring seal at the top of the chamber section is worn. Renew it if necessary.

A push-button or 'European' cistern

Many modern slimline WC cisterns are supplied by a Torbeck valve – a modified diaphragm type with a very short float arm and miniature float (below) – or an ingenious vertical valve with a float cup that fits round the central column of the valve body. Both are very quiet in operation, although the float-cup valve can be slow to refill the cistern if it is supplied with water from a storage tank, rather than being plumbed in directly to the mains.

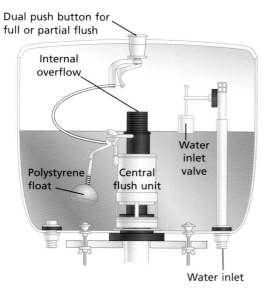

Dual push button for full or partial flush

Internal overflow

Polystyrene float

Central flush unit

Water inlet valve

Water inlet

In these slimline cisterns, a plastic valve-operated flush mechanism is activated by a push button in the cistern lid. The mechanism also incorporates an integral overflow, and if the inlet valve fails for any reason, the water flows over the centre of the flush unit into the toilet bowl. This will be noticed as constantly running water in the toilet bowl and should be repaired as soon as possible.

The push button is in two parts (below) and is linked to a plunger to operate the flush, rather than the conventional wire link and float arm of a traditional flushing mechanism.

Replacing the seat

Replacing a broken or ugly old toilet seat can revitalise a WC. Choose from a wide range of styles to suit your bathroom.

1 Undo the plastic wing-nuts under the rear of the toilet bowl and remove the broken seat. Clean around the bolt holes and make sure the area is rinsed properly and dry. Place the new seat in position.

2 Make sure the supplied washers are fitted above and below the bowl, on both bolts. Finger-tighten the wing-nuts. Then check the seat is centred on the bowl. Tighten the nuts fully.

Descaling the shower head

If the flow of water from a shower head is weak or uneven, the holes in the rose are probably blocked with limescale.

1 Unscrew the shower head. There may be a tool supplied with your shower; use a screwdriver if there is a central screw. If the rose does not unscrew, remove the whole head from the hose. Pour white vinegar or descaler through or over the shower head.

2 Scrub the rose with an old nailbrush or washing-up brush. If the holes are badly blocked, soak the head in a proprietary descaler according to the manufacturer's instructions or leave it overnight in undiluted distilled white vinegar.

3 Reattach the shower head to the hose, and turn the shower on for a few minutes on its cold setting to rinse out the limescale and remaining descaler or vinegar. Repeat this process several times to make sure all the cleaning product has been thoroughly rinsed away.

Repairing a pull-cord

A pull-cord may break at the point where it emerges from the switch. You don't need to replace the whole fitting – just buy a new cord.

Tools *Screwdriver; electrician's insulated screwdriver; scissors.*

Materials *Replacement cord. Possibly green-and-yellow earth sleeving.*

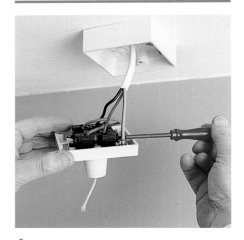

1 Turn off the power to the lighting circuit at the consumer unit. Loosen the screws securing the switch to its mounting box and pull it away. Note which cable core goes to which terminal on the switch baseplate, and then disconnect the cable cores from their terminals.

2 Remove the four screws securing the body of the switch to the back of the faceplate. Hold the two together as you do this to prevent the spring inside sending bits everywhere as you release the screws.

5 Make a knot at one end of the new cord, then thread the other end through the washer and the slot in the nylon peg. Feed the cord down through the spring and put the nylon peg back in. The wings on the side of the peg engage in the grooves beside the spring. Put the shaft with the on/off markings back in place.

3 Lift off the body and examine how the switch works. In the example here, each pull of the cord turns the shaft with on/off markings 90° and makes or breaks the contacts within the switch.

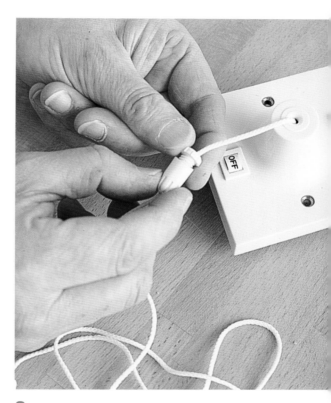

4 Lift off the shaft with on/off markings so you can remove the nylon peg to which the pull-cord is attached. Leave the spring where it is. Make a note of the position of any small washers on the cord.

6 Put the two parts of the switch together and replace the screws. Thread the cord through the fitting that connects it to the rest of the pull-cord, and knot it. Reconnect the circuit cable. If the earth core is bare, fit green-and-yellow PVC earth sleeving over it beforehand. Fit the switch back on its box.

Fitting a new kitchen

Planning a new kitchen

The kitchen is one of the most-used rooms in the house, so if you intend to replace yours it is worth spending time planning the content and layout of your new space.

There must be at least 600mm directly above a hob, although it is best to avoid siting units here if you can. Try to use this space only for an extractor fan, which should be between 600 and 915mm above the hob.

Start by drawing up a wish list of all the things you would like to incorporate and try to plan around those. Sketch out a scale plan of the room on graph paper and draw in where you would like the oven, fridge and other key appliances to go, then fit the other cabinets around this.

Don't plan your kitchen to fit exactly between two walls. It will be much easier to fit if you allow for a little tolerance at either end – walls are seldom completely flat and it is very difficult to cut down a unit by a tiny amount in order to squeeze it into a very tight space.

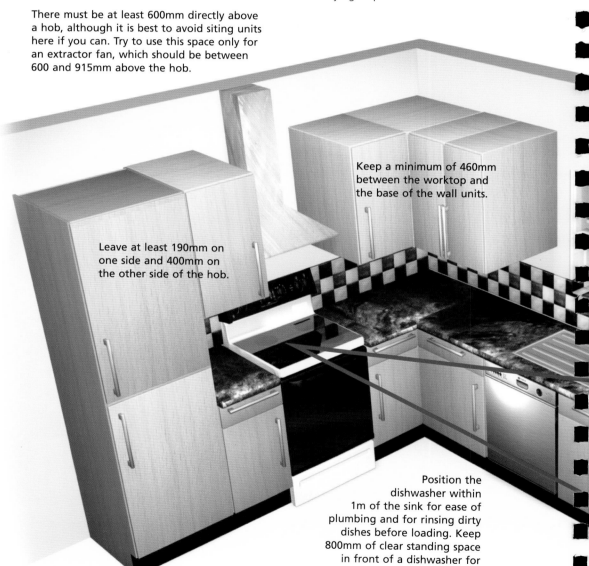

Keep a minimum of 460mm between the worktop and the base of the wall units.

Leave at least 190mm on one side and 400mm on the other side of the hob.

Position the dishwasher within 1m of the sink for ease of plumbing and for rinsing dirty dishes before loading. Keep 800mm of clear standing space in front of a dishwasher for easy loading.

The working triangle

Kitchens tend to work best when they follow the 'working triangle' principle. Try to position the main food storage and preparation area, the cooker, and the sink in a triangle, spaced equally apart and with a total distance between them of no more than 7.5m. A kitchen will be frustrating to use if you have to walk a long way between the fridge and the cooker or double back time and again every time you so much as make a cup of tea.

HELPFUL TIP

Freestanding appliances are sometimes larger than those designed to be fitted into a kitchen. You may need a deeper length of worktop to come out to the front edge of a washing machine, for example.

If you plan to tile the splashback between the worktop and the units, try to position the units so that you can fit a whole number of tiles, to save you cutting each tile in the top or bottom row.

Allow at least 450mm on one side and 600mm on the other side of the sink to give room for stacking clean and dirty pans when washing up.

Planning the work

• Solid flooring, such as stone or ceramic tiles, should be fitted before the units. This is the best way to achieve a good finish, but does mean that you pay for flooring you never see, underneath the units. Vinyl can be laid after the units and tucked under the plinths at their base.
• Consider adding halogen spots or strip lights beneath wall units to illuminate the work surface. Plan the wiring before you install the units if you want the lights to run from a single switch on the main lighting circuit.
• Run any cables or pipes to their new position before you start fitting units, when you have clear access to all the walls and the floor.
• Venting extractor fans must be fitted with ducting leading to an external wall. If the ducting is more than 5m long, the fan is unlikely to be powerful enough to expel any air. In this case, choose a recirculating model, which does not need venting to the outdoors.
• Worktops should overhang the cabinets beneath by about 20mm when the doors are in place. Most base units are 570mm deep, so a standard 600mm worktop will be a good fit, with a little tolerance for scribing it to match an uneven wall along the back edge.

Next to the opening side of the fridge, try to leave at least 400mm of worktop space.

The minimum required space between an island unit and the surrounding units is 1.2m, so that cupboard doors on both sides can be open at once.

Most modern kitchens are fitted or built in. A hob and sink are integrated within a run of cupboards and drawers, and topped by a length of work surface that unifies the whole room (left). A well-designed layout makes for an efficient use of space and easy cleaning. By and large, kitchen manufacturers produce a range of standard 'carcasses' or units to which you fit your choice of doors and drawer fronts.

Freestanding units Instead of having a fully fitted kitchen, you could opt for several separate items of furniture – a dresser, a butcher's block, a range cooker, an 'island' food preparation area in the centre of the room – or a combination of coordinated fitted and freestanding pieces (above). A mixture of furniture styles can look untidy, while narrow gaps between freestanding items may be hard to clean.

Choosing a style of kitchen

Rustic country farmhouse or granite-and-stainless steel modern? Fitted or freestanding? With such a vast range of styles and finishes available, choosing a kitchen has never been more challenging – or more fun.

Door and drawer fronts Kitchen furniture needs to look good and withstand a lot of wear and tear. The less expensive doors are made of veneered chipboard – the veneer may be natural wood, a painted finish or even stainless steel. One of the latest innovations is a high gloss finish in a solid colour. The more expensive ranges usually have solid wood doors – with a waxed, varnished, limed or painted finish. The door profile may be a simple Shaker style (left), or incorporate traditional panels (above) or tongue-and-groove for a farmhouse effect.

Choosing handles

You can affect the whole look and feel of a kitchen simply by changing the handles on the cupboards and drawers.

Ornate metal An antiqued brass or bronze finish in a decorative style looks stunning with these painted wooden doors – perfect in a period kitchen. But replace these with a brushed steel 'D'-shaped handle and the effect would instantly be 21st century. Simple wooden knobs on the same painted cupboards, however, would hint 'Shaker'.

Knobs These are the most basic handles. Easy to fit or to change, knobs are available in wood – from cherry to oak; metals – including polished brass, bronze, pewter, chrome or stainless steel; or even porcelain.

Bar handles Stainless steel bar handles are available in different thicknesses for a variety of effects. They are also available in various lengths from less than 200mm to a striking 'design statement' metre-plus. Measure accurately before fitting – any error will look disastrous.

Worktops

Laminate is the most widely used worktop material. It is hardwearing, easy to fit and comes in hundreds of textures and finishes – including wood-effect and glossy mock granite. It is relatively inexpensive.

Granite is an increasingly popular material for worktops. It is tough and glossy, and, beside the sink, can have draining grooves machined into it. It should be supplied and fitted by a specialist. It is costly, but becoming more competitive.

Hardwood looks beautiful but must be protected from water and spills with regular applications of oil. It is relatively expensive but improves with age.

Stainless steel (below) can be customised to any shape or size, with sink bowls and drainers seamlessly welded and polished into the worktop. It is sleek and hygienic but shows every fingerprint. It is an expensive option.

Acrylic blends such as Corian® are manufactured in the form of sheets and sinks. A sink with machined drainage grooves can be custom made as part of a continuous worktop. These composites are available in numerous colours. They are very hardwearing but can be costly.

Clever storage

There is no reason, in a modern kitchen, to waste time on your knees searching for items in the murky depths at the back of a cupboard. Kitchen manufacturers produce a vast range of accessories to answer every storage need. You can store wine in special bottle storage drawers. Flexible cutlery trays and utensil dividers can be organised in various layouts. Some cutlery trays have adjustable handle supports to provide secure storage even for large knives. How about a pull-out chopping board or ironing board? Both these items can be installed in the drawer space of most standard base cabinets. As you open the 'drawer', supports automatically extend.

Filling gaps If standard units don't fill the available space, make use of the deep, narrow gaps by fitting extendible tea towel rails, or creating a space to store trays.

Pull-out larder Available in various heights and widths, larder units protrude into the room a full length of the runner when pulled from the cabinet (above right).

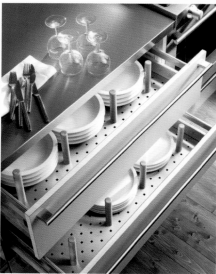

Plate drawers There are two types of plate drawer available. One has deep grooves allowing plates to be stored upright, rather like a draining rack; the other has adjustable dividers for the flat storage of stacks of plates of different diameters (above). These drawers may have a rubber liner to stop china from slipping when the drawer is pulled out.

Drawer shelves These come in various sizes and depths. Wire basket drawers, which allow air to circulate, make ideal vegetable storage, especially for potatoes and onions. Heavy duty drawer shelves (left) are strong enough to support the weight of tinned goods and jars of provisions.

Carousels and corner units Wirework carousels are worth considering in corner units. Each basket can be turned

independently, affording a good view of stored items on both upper and lower shelf levels. Another effective system is the 'magic corner' (above): as you open the door the first set of baskets swings out pulling the second set along. This system is slightly harder to install than a carousel.

Worktop rail Chrome or stainless steel rails are good looking and practical. Simply hang kitchen utensils, sieves and colanders from the hooks supplied.

Pull-out waste With recycling in mind, separate kitchen waste into a series of bins concealed in a drawer or cupboard (right).

Appliances and fittings

When designing a kitchen from scratch, you need to think carefully about the appliances it must incorporate. You may be lucky enough to have a utility room for your washing machine, tumble dryer and perhaps a deep freeze. If not, then these appliances, along with the cooker and cooker hood, fridge and dishwasher have all got to be fitted in to what may not be the largest room in the house.

Cooker hoods Steam from cooking can cause wet walls and furniture and make for an unpleasant atmosphere in the kitchen. It can even cause mould to form and warp units. Strong smells spread throughout the house and vapourised cooking oils are deposited on surfaces near the hob. The most effective cooker hoods are ducted outside, and extract most of the steam and smells; their replaceable filters collect airborne grease. But even if you cannot fit an extraction duct, modern re-circulating hoods do a pretty good job. These contain a charcoal filter (which needs replacing regularly) that collects airborne grease, dissipates steam and weakens cooking smells. Hood styles include modern 'chimneys' (right); integrated cooker hoods that match the units; slimline recirculating ones that fit beneath a wall unit; and wider models specially designed for ranges.

Fitted hobs and ovens Hobs are sold in both gas and electric versions. If you don't have a gas supply to your home, you can buy a gas hob for use with replaceable cylinders. Electric hobs have sealed plates or ceramic tops. Fitted ovens are housed in low or high level units that come as part of a fitted kitchen. These can also incorporate a double oven, grill and microwave.

Freestanding cookers A freestanding cooker can stand alone or be installed as part of a fitted kitchen. If you cook for a large family, a range-style cooker with two ovens, four or more rings, a griddle and a plate warmer can be a good option. Many cooks like the practicality of an eye-level grill and choose a cooker with this feature – though in terms of kitchen design, a low level cooker gives a more streamlined look.

Integrated appliances Most kitchen appliances come in standard sizes and are designed to slot neatly under the worktop. Some appliances, including fridges, fridge-freezers and dishwashers, can be supplied with special doors to which you fit a fascia that matches the units (right), creating an integrated, unbroken run.

Plinth heaters Plinth or 'kickspace' heaters fit into the space beneath a base unit and feed warmed air through special grilles fitted into the kick-plate. One type is a simple electric fan heater. Another type connects to the central heating system and blows hot air into the kitchen when the central heating is on. Best of all is a combination heater: this is connected to the central heating but also has an electric element – ideal for quickly warming up a cold kitchen when the central heating is not switched on. There may also be a 'summer/winter' switch, which provides a fan-only option for warm weather.

Taps The right tap can add real charisma to the kitchen. If you are aiming for an ultra modern look, a minimalist mixer will do the job – but a 'farmhouse' kitchen demands a more traditional tap. Do you want a dual-flow tap, which provides independent hot and cold water flow, or a single lever tap, which combines hot and cold water with one adjustment? Curved high neck taps (right) look elegant and are practical too for filling a kettle or bucket. Here, the third lever supplies filtered drinking water from a unit plumbed in under the sink. Some mixer taps have a pull-out head. A single lever controls the water temperature and the pull-out spray head, which is mounted in the body of the tap, allows you to wash individual items or rinse out the sink itself.

Under-cupboard lighting Lights fixed to the undersides of wall units can create useful illumination for the cook as well as providing ambient lighting when the main room lights are switched off. Installing a simple fluorescent tube, or a fitting that incorporates a row of spotlights, is a straightforward DIY job. If the cupboards are already in place, these fittings can be plugged into an existing socket and the cable clipped to the underside of the units. If you are starting from scratch, or bridging a gap between two units, consider chasing the cables into the wall.

Planning the job

Think about how long the job is going to take you and how you will cook and wash up during the work. It may be best to tackle the kitchen refit in stages.

You may have to wait for weeks or even months for your kitchen units to arrive once you have placed your order, so resist the temptation to start demolishing your old kitchen too soon.

Plan the layout Spend time thinking carefully about your layout and whether you could improve on the existing arrangement (pages 42–43). Most kitchen suppliers will be happy to help you with this and many use computer software to draw up plans and 3D projections of how your new kitchen will look to help you to decide on the arrangement that will be best for your needs.

Services Think about where the gas supply, if you have one, comes into the kitchen, where water supply and drainage pipes run and where your electrical sockets are positioned. If you need to move a gas supply, this must be done by a CORGI-registered engineer. Plumbing can be re-routed once the old units have been removed. And while the old tiles are off the wall electrical sockets can be added or moved to more appropriate positions.

Ventilation Think about whether you can position your cooker against an external wall so that the extractor fan can vent directly to the outside. If not, you will need to order a recirculating model, with a charcoal filter.

Appliances Decide whether you would like free-standing or integrated appliances, and think about which appliances you need. Be sure to order these at the same time as the kitchen units, or in plenty of time to coordinate their delivery.

Lighting A complete refit offers an ideal opportunity to improve the lighting in a dingy kitchen. Think about where your food preparation and cooking areas will be and consider how best to illuminate them with ceiling and under-cupboard lights.

ORDER OF WORK

• **Remove existing units**, leaving a couple in place with a short section of worktop if necessary as a temporary kitchen while you work.
• **Remove tiles** from the walls.
• **Lift flooring.** Fill any holes in the subfloor or lay a screed over the whole floor to create a new level surface to work from.

• **Re-route electrics** if necessary. All wiring work must be checked to be sure that it conforms with Building Regulations (see page 20). Make good any chases cut in the walls for new cable runs.
• **Re-route plumbing** supply and drainage pipes if necessary. Work that affects the main soil stack may be subject to Building Control Regulations – check with your local council (see page 20).
• **Lay new flooring** if you are using ceramic or stone tiles or solid wood.
• **Install wall units**
• **Install base units**
• **Cut worktop** for an inset sink and for joints at corners. Fit worktops and secure to base units.
• **Fit sink** and complete other plumbing to taps, drains and appliances.
• **Lay new flooring** if you are using vinyl, floor tiles or laminate boards.
• **Install electrical appliances** such as an integrated fridge freezer or cooker.
• **Fit extractor fan** and run vent pipe to outside if appropriate.
• **Decorate** with paint and tiles.

Removing ceramic tiles

Leaving tiles in place and painting or tiling over them is often the easiest option, but if you want a flat finish for painting or wallpapering or you want to run cable to new electrical sockets the tiles must be removed.

Tiles in older houses may be stuck to the wall with cement mortar – sometimes 15mm thick. If you remove them you will probably need to have the wall plastered before you can decorate. Tiles stuck with adhesive are easier to get off, but they may pull plaster with them. In this case, the surface will need to be made good.

Tools *Heavy duty gloves; safety goggles; dust mask; wide steel masonry chisel (bolster); club hammer; paint scraper. Possibly also: power sander.*

Before you start Put on protective clothing – splinters of glass from the glaze will fly in all directions as you work. Close doors to prevent dust escaping from the room.

1 Prise the tiles away from the wall one at a time with a bolster chisel and a club hammer. Some will come away in one piece, others may crack and break. There is no easy technique – continue to chisel until you have removed all of the tiles.

2 Use a sharp paint or wallpaper scraper to remove any adhesive left on the wall. If the tiles were stuck with cement mortar you will need to continue chipping with the bolster chisel.

TAKING UP OLD FLOORINGS

Old tiles and parquet that are firmly stuck can form a sound base for a new floor. But carpets and sheet vinyls – and any other flooring that is not well stuck down – must be removed before you lay a new one.

A garden spade is an excellent tool for lifting a floor covering such as vinyl tiles or lino, when the glue is not holding well. Its blade has a sharp edge that you can push under the material (file it sharper if necessary) and the long handle allows plenty or leverage for lifting. For a large area, hire a powered floor-tile stripper.

Old quarry tiles are difficult to remove, and may only reveal an unsatisfactory sub-floor underneath. It is probably best to leave them in place. If a few tiles are damaged or missing, remove damaged pieces with a bolster and club hammer – wearing safety goggles. Then replace them with new tiles, or fill the gaps with sand and cement.

If a quarry-tiled floor is in a very bad state, clear out badly broken and crumbling patches, clean thoroughly, fill deeper holes with sand and cement, and then apply a self-levelling compound to the entire floor. This will give a sound smooth base for laying your chosen finished flooring material.

Repositioning the services

Run new cables and pipework while the room is empty, but measure carefully to be sure to terminate them in the correct places.

Preparing a route for a cable

1 Hold the mounting box in position. For a socket outlet it should be at least 150mm above worktop level. For a light switch, it should be at about shoulder height. Draw a line round it as a guide.

2 Using a masonry bit, drill holes round the marked outline to the depth of the box. Drill more holes within the marked area. **Alternatively** Use a proprietary plastic drilling jig, which creates a honeycomb effect that is easy to chop out.

3 Cut out the recess to the required depth with a brick bolster and club hammer.

4 Plan the route for the cable. It should run vertically above or below a socket outlet or switch. A horizontal run should be close to the ceiling or the skirting board. Never run it diagonally.

5 Mark the route with two lines 25mm apart. Avoid making sharp bends, wherever possible.

6 Check with a cable detector along the route to make sure that you are not going to interfere with any cables or pipes buried in the wall. If you are at all uncertain whether there is live wiring near the spot where you are working, switch off at the mains until you have made sure.

7 When you know that the route is safe, use a sharp knife to score along both edges of the chase. Use a cold chisel and club hammer to cut out the plaster. Protect your eyes with safety goggles.
Alternatively Hire an electric chasing machine to cut out the chase.

8 Check that the length of the chase is deep enough for the oval PVC conduit to fit easily. If it is too near the surface, only a skim of plaster or filler will cover it when you make good and it will probably crack. A covering of 5mm of plaster or filler over the conduit should be thick enough to stay sound and prevent cracking.

9 Feed the cable into the conduit and secure it in the chase with galvanised nails on each side. Leave enough spare cable at each end of the run to reach the mounting boxes easily. Ease the end of the cable or cables through the grommet into the mounting box. Slide the box into the recess and screw it into the wall behind.

Routes in plasterboard

Cable can be run in the cavity within a stud partition wall. You will have to cut notches in the frame.

1 Use a bradawl to locate the frame, or a wiring detector to locate the rows of nails holding the plasterboard to the frame.

2 With a sharp knife, cut away a section of plasterboard about 120mm square wherever your planned route crosses a frame member.

3 Chisel a groove in the exposed frame to hold the cable easily.

4 If you are running a spur cable from an existing socket to another further along the worktop, you are likely to be feeding the

cable horizontally. Push the cable along between the plasterboard panels. At each upright, draw out a loop of cable long enough to reach the next upright. Feed it along and set it in the prepared groove.

5 When the cable is in the required position, fix it to the timbers with clips.

6 Cut new squares of plasterboard to replace the sections cut away. Tack them securely to the timbers at top and bottom, keeping the tacks well clear of the cable. Fill round the patches with interior filler.

Fitting a plastic mounting box

Knock out the most convenient holes for the cable or cables to enter the mounting box. Hold the box in position, check with a spirit level that it is horizontal and draw a line round it. Cut away the marked section of plasterboard with a sharp knife. Feed the cable or cables into the box. Push the mounting box into the hole. Some boxes have spring-loaded fixing clips which simply snap into place as you push the box in; others have retractable lugs which you push out to hold the box. Prepare the conductors and connect them to the terminals on the accessory faceplate. Screw the faceplate to the box.

Moving plumbing pipes

Turn off the water supply (page 23) before you start working on existing pipes. Ways of joining pipes are covered on pages 66–67, but you may need to bend copper pipes to go round corners or negotiate awkward features in your room. Bending the pipe is a better option than fitting a series of elbows and joints. Each joint will reduce the water pressure fractionally and is prone to leak. Using flexible plastic pipe and speedfit joints is a quick and easy way of running supply pipes to new positions. Never try to bend rigid copper piping by hand without a spring to support the pipe walls – the pipe will kink at the bend if it is not supported.

Bending copper piping with a spring

1 If the pipe is longer than the spring, tie string to the spring end.

2 Grease the spring well with petroleum jelly and push it into the pipe.

3 Bend the pipe across your knee with gentle hand pressure to the required angle.

4 Overbend the pipe a little more, then ease it gently back again. This action helps to free the spring and makes it easier to withdraw.

5 Insert a screwdriver blade through the spring loop. Twist the spring to reduce its diameter, then pull it out.

Bending with a machine

1 Clamp the pipe against the correct-sized semicircular former. Place the guide block of the correct diameter between the pipe and the movable handle.

2 Squeeze the handles together until the pipe is curved to the required angle round the semicircular former.

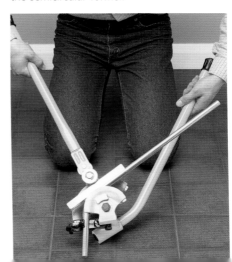

Assembling kitchen units

Put the cabinets together one at a time to avoid muddling parts. All the bits might look the same but there are often differences from unit to unit.

1 Take all the components out of the box and check them against the list of contents. If anything is missing, check the box and all the packaging again.

2 Screw or hammer in the fixings to the inside of the side panels.

3 If the wall unit is to be hung from brackets, fit the cupboard section of the bracket now. Some units are assembled fully and then screwed directly to the wall.

4 Slot the cam part of the cam and screw fixing into the adjacent panel and then slide it into place, tapping it down gently if necessary to get a tight fit.

5 Slide the back panel into place then complete the assembly of the other two sides.

Self-assembly fixings for flat-pack kitchens

Some kitchens are supplied as flat-pack units that must be assembled on site. Each unit will be individually packed, with its own special fixings in the box, and fixing holes already drilled in the appropriate places. Here are the two most common fixings that you are likely to encounter.

Dowels Standard dowels are 25–30mm long, and are glued in place. Like the majority of the fixings used in flat pack furniture they are tapped into factory-made pre-drilled holes. Although simple they are very effective and give a strong concealed joint.

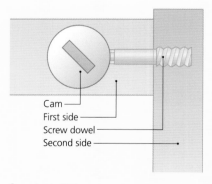

Cam —
First side —
Screw dowel —
Second side —

Cam lock fittings

This fastening is for joining two panels together. The cam is dropped into a shallow recess on the face of one part and a screw with a pronounced head or a steel screw dowel is driven into a pre-drilled hole in the other part to be joined.
The head of the screw passes through a clearance hole in the first part and into the cam. Turning the cam 90° clockwise tightens the joint.

Installing the kitchen units

Preparation is key to a good finish. Spend time measuring and marking before you position the first cabinet and the job will be easier and better in the long run.

1 Establish a datum line, a line that you know is level and correctly positioned and that you can work from when positioning the units. Measure up the wall to 890mm (the height of a base unit) and use a spirit level or laser level to transfer this line around the room.

2 Check the measurement around the room to make sure that the floor does not dip or rise significantly. Adjust the line until you have a level that all the units will sit at.

3 Use a spirit level to draw perpendicular lines up the wall from your datum to help you to position the wall units plumb. Mark a second horizontal line at the level of the

FIXING WALL UNITS TO STUD PARTITION WALLS

Wall units can be fixed to stud walls using fixings for hollow walls, but once the cupboards are fully loaded, they will be very heavy, so it is wise to reinforce the fixing area. Cut out a strip of plasterboard the length of the run of the units and 100mm wide at the position where the fixings will be made. Take care not to cut through the studs. Replace the plasterboard with a length of 100 x 25mm softwood, firmly fixed to the partition studs. Notch the bearer over the studs.

tops of your wall units and then measure down to mark the positions of their fixing brackets, if they use them.

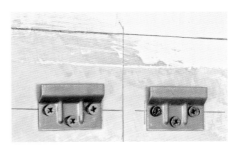

4 Drill and fix the brackets, using heavy-duty metal toggle fixings for a strong fix in a stud wall.

SAFETY TIP

Most base units come with legs that can be screwed in or out to adjust the height of the unit and to level it. Never extend the legs to their full length as they will be weakened. If your floor is very uneven, pack under the feet with pieces of wood and use the legs to make fine adjustments.

Fitting the base units

1 Once all the wall brackets are in position start with the first base unit. It is crucial to make this level and plumb, as all the other units will work off this.

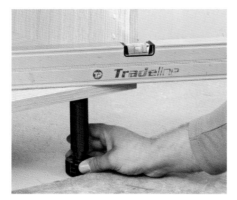

2 Move the cupboard into position then use a spirit level to check that it is level in all directions. Adjust the cupboard legs, by turning them to screw in or out to make them shorter or longer.

3 Once you are happy with the position of the first unit, move on to the next. Level each cupboard with the one next to it then clamp them together, drill two pilot holes through the sides and screw the units together. Use 30mm screws to join standard 18mm carcasses, or shorter ones if your carcasses are thinner 15mm ones.

4 Where plumbing pipes need to come into the units, use a hole saw to drill through the back of the cupboard. Move the cupboard into place and mark the position of the pipes. Cut the holes.

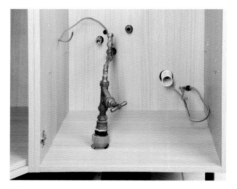

5 Manoeuvre the unit into position and fix it into place. It is sometimes also necessary to use a jigsaw to take a notch out of the side panels of units where a waste pipe runs behind and cannot fit in the space behind the units.

6 Once you have a run of cupboards in place, fix them back to the wall. The cupboards may be supplied with brackets for this, or you may need to screw through the back rail directly into the wall. Drill and plug holes in the wall, re-check the levelling of the cupboards if you have moved them to do so and screw them home.

Hanging the wall units

1 Some wall units fix directly to the wall by screwing through holes in the back panel of the cupboard straight into plugs driven into the wall, but most use adjustable brackets, that allow you to tweak the alignments of the cupboards once you have a run in place.

4 Once all the cupboards are positioned, slide the decorative covers into place over the brackets.

2 Carefully lift the first cupboard into position and hook the catches that are part of the cupboard-mounted brackets over the wall-mounted brackets that you fixed in position earlier.

Fitting cornice, pelmet and plinths

Many kitchens come with a decorative finishing strip of coordinating cornice around the top edges of the wall units and a pelmet strip that finishes the bottom edge of the wall units, helping to hide under-cupboard strip lights.

Fitting cornice

3 Loosely screw in the brackets to hold the cupboard steady until the whole run of units is in position, then tighten the fixings in turn so that the cupboards are secure and all level with one another. On the fixings shown here, adjusting the top screw on the bracket lifts the cupboards up and down and the bottom screw pulls them into the wall or moves them slightly away. Different brands may vary.

1 Offer up a length of cornice to the cupboards and mark a cutting point for the mitred corner. Make a mark where the bottom edge of the cornice meets the outer edge of the cupboard's carcass.

EXPERT JOINTS

If you are fitting cornice and pelmet to your kitchen it may be worth hiring a bench-mounted mitre saw, for a day to help you to make precise cuts for a professional finish. Always wear safety goggles and ear defenders and pay close attention to the safety instructions.

2 Line up the cutting mark with the blade. If the joint is for a 90° corner, you will need to make a 45° cut on each of the joining pieces. If the cornice is to trim a diagonal corner cupboard each angle is 135°, so make two 67.5° cuts. A mitre saw makes it easy to set up these cuts.

3 Hold the cornice flat and firm on the saw's cutting plate and make the cuts.

4 MDF trim should be joined with a 2-part mitre kit, which gives a stronger and much faster bond than PVA glue. Spray activator on one piece, spread adhesive on the other piece, then carefully bring them together to make a neat join and hold them for 10 seconds, until the joint is set. If the cornice is solid wood, join the pieces with PVA wood glue or a fast grip-fix adhesive.

5 Lift the cornice into place along the top edge of the units. Drill through the cornice into the cupboard tops and screw the trim into position.

Fitting lighting pelmet

1 Measure, cut and join lengths of the pelmet in the same way as for cornice. Align the face of the pelmet with the front edge of the cupboard carcasses.

2 Fix the pelmet to the base of the cupboards using plastic block joints. Drill pilot holes into the pelmet then screw blocks to the pelmet at 500mm intervals using 25mm screws.

3 Offer up the pelmet to the cupboard and clamp it in place temporarily.

4 Drill pilot holes up into the base of the cupboards and screw the block connectors to the units using 25mm screws. Remove the clamps.

Fitting plinths

Some kitchens have decorative legs and are designed to have a free-standing look, but most are finished along the bottom edge with a strip of plinth that clips to the cupboard legs.

1 Cut the plinth to length. At a 90° corner, allow one length to extend under the cupboards and butt the adjoining length to it. For angled cupboards, cut mitred joints, as for cornice and lighting pelmet.

2 Lay the cut lengths of plinth on the floor in front of the cupboards and mark the centre positions of the cupboard legs. Fix the clips to the centre of the plinth, matching the position of the legs they are to clip to.

3 The plinth will be supplied with iron-on edging tape to finish cut edges where they are visible at the end of a run of cupboards.

EXPERT TIP

Some makes of kitchen now offer 'soft-closing' hinges, similar to the self-closing drawers that have been available for some time. A simple plastic piston clips onto one hinge of each cupboard. This prevents the door from being slammed, slowing it down to a gentle close, with no banging.

Fitting doors and handles

Many units come with the hinges already fixed to the doors and cupboards, making fitting simple. Fixings for drawer fronts vary from kitchen to kitchen. Follow the manufacturer's instructions.

Hanging doors

Even if the hinges are not pre-fitted, the holes will be drilled for them and it is a simple job to fit them in position on both door and unit.

1 Lift the doors into position, sliding and clicking the arm of the hinge into the bracket on the cupboard.

2 Tighten the screws to hold the door then close it. Make sure that the door opens and closes without catching on the adjacent door and check that it is aligned with the cupboard and the doors on either side of it.

3 Use the screws on the hinges to adjust the position of the door as necessary. The top and bottom screws move the door up and down. The screw nearest to the door pushes the door away from the cupboard or tightens it up. And the screw furthest from the door moves the door from left to right when it is closed.

Fitting handles

Your doors and drawer fronts may come pre-drilled with holes to suit the accompanying handles, but since a variety of handles is usually available for each kitchen style you will probably need to position and fix them yourself.

1 Decide where you would like the handles to sit on the door. This may be dictated by the style of the door, centring handles within a frame around the edge of a door, for example. Measure and mark the position of the holes on the face of each door, being careful to be consistent, so that all the handles are perfectly aligned.

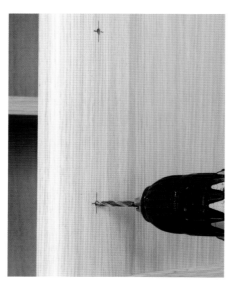

2 Drill through the door from the front, holding a block of wood behind the hole to prevent the inner face of the door from splitting as the drill breaks through the finish.

3 Screw the handles into place from the inside of the door.

Cutting a laminate worktop to fit

Granite is an increasingly popular material for kitchen worktops, but fitting it is a job for the professionals. Getting a good finish matching the pattern of solid wood blockboard worktop can also be tricky, but fitting laminate tops is a simple DIY task with the right equipment.

EXPERT TIP

To do a professional job of fitting your worktop it is worth hiring a router and worktop cutting jig. The jig is a template for cutting the mitre joint, giving you a perfect tight joint when the pieces are brought together – something that is very difficult to achieve without the jig's help. You will also need a sturdy pair of trestles.

Cutting the worktops

1 Measure off the front of the cupboards to the wall to check the maximum depth around the kitchen. Standard worktops are 600mm deep, which allows a little extra depth to scribe the back edge to the profile of the wall if it is not square (see page 61).

2 Lay two lengths of worktop in position, overlapping one on top of the other and mark where they meet at the front edge.

3 Clamp the first length of worktop to a pair of trestles and then clamp the jig in place on the worktop. Make sure that you get the jig the right way up, selecting the correct angle for your cut. If you are making a 90° joint, position the sharper 45° angle at the front edge of the worktop. The jig will come with full instructions for correct positioning. Follow them carefully: making a mistake cutting a length of worktop can be expensive.

4 Use the router to cut the worktop, following the line of the jig and making several passes with the tool, cutting deeper each time. Always wear ear defenders and goggles when using the router.

5 The jig will also have a template for cutting slots in the underside of the worktop to hold the bolts that will join the pieces together. Turn the worktop over and clamp the jig into position. On a standard worktop, you will have three bolts along each cut edge to make the join secure.

6 Set the depth of the router to around half the depth of the worktop and cut out the slots.

Scribing to fit an uneven wall

1 Lift the worktops into position on the cupboards, one at a time. Slight gaps along the back edge where the wall is not square will normally be hidden by the thickness of any wall tiles or decorative upstand you plan to fit.

2 Measure the overhang at the front edge, measuring off the carcass, not the cupboard doors, which might not be perfectly square. Position the worktop with an even overhang all the way along – 40mm is the standard overhang, but it can be more or slightly less if your measurements are not quite the same.

3 If the wall is very out of true, measure the largest gap between the worktop and the wall and scribe the worktop to trim this amount off the back edge. Set a pair of compasses to the measurement of the gap and drag them along the wall, drawing a cutting line the length of the worktop.

4 Use a jigsaw to cut the worktop to your line, then slide the worktops back into position and check the fit.

FINISHING OFF

Imperfect joins along the back of a worktop will probably be hidden by the depth of tiles, if you are tiling splashbacks along the walls. They can also be disguised by a strip of wood moulding, called an upstand, fixed in the angle between the worktop and the wall and finished with a bead of sealant. Wood mouldings look particularly effective as a finishing touch to a wooden worktop.

Fitting an inset sink

An inset sink with an integral draining board to one side is the most common choice and the best option for use with laminate worktops.

1 Place the upturned sink on the worktop. Make sure you have it the correct way round for your taps and drainer. Some sinks are supplied with a cutting template. If your worktops are dark, stick a wide strip of masking tape where you are going to cut so that your pencil marks will be visible.

2 Carefully measure to ensure that the bowl of the sink will fall within the cupboard beneath and that it will not foul on the sides – you may need to cut away part of the bracing piece that runs across the top of some units. A one and a half bowl sink is a tight fit in a standard 600mm unit, so take care to measure accurately.

3 Make sure that the sink is parallel with the front edge of the worktop. Measure back 60mm from the front edge to allow

---

EXPERT TIP

A jigsaw with a downward pointing blade will not chip the surface of the worktop as a standard up-cutting one can, but it is harder to make a vertical cut through the thick worktop. You may need to neaten the edges with a sander, but the finish at the surface will be better.

---

for a worktop overhang and the thickness of the cupboard carcass. Mark the corners of the sink. Measure in 10mm (do not cut to the edge of the sink – the hole must be slightly smaller) and use a straightedge to join up the marks for a cutting line.

4 Drill 10mm holes in each corner. This makes a smooth radius at the corners and allows room for a jigsaw to be inserted.

5 Use a jigsaw with a downward cutting blade (see Expert Tip) to cut out the hole.

6 Paint PVA glue onto the cut edge to seal it and run a bead of silicone mastic around the underside lip of the sink, then drop the sink into position. Some sinks are supplied with a gasket to fit between the sink and the worktop.

7 Use the clips supplied with the sink to secure it to the worktop.

8 If you have trestles to work on, you may find it easier to fix the taps to the sink before you install the worktop. This will minimise the work you have to do from inside the cupboard.

9 You can also fit the plughole and waste traps, leaving only the final connections to make once the worktop is installed.

SAFETY WARNING

Metal sinks, taps and pipes within kitchen cupboards must be bonded into the house's main earthing system. They could be a danger if they come into contact with a conductor carrying current or if an electrical fault occurs. Run 4mm² earth cable from a clamp attached

to the fitting to the earth terminal block in the consumer unit.

Fixing and finishing the worktop

Once the worktops are cut they can be fitted to the units.

1 Position a length of worktop on top of the units. Push it back to the wall and then adjust it to make sure that it is parallel with the front edge of the units (not the doors, which may not be perfectly square) and with an even overhang of around 40mm.

2 If the worktop butts up to another piece then join the two pieces together before securing them to the cupboards. Run a bead of silicone mastic along one cut edge then work from the underside to bolt the pieces together.

3 Position the joining bolts in the slots cut earlier and tighten the nuts to pull the pieces together. Wipe away any excess silicone that has been squeezed out of the gap. Drive a 40mm screw up through the top rail of each cupboard into the worktop.

Fitting an edging strip

Finish the cut edges of a laminate worktop with the edging strip that is supplied.

1 Cut a piece roughly to length, hold it in position and draw around the bullnose shape at the front edge. Cut roughly but not precisely to this line – the strip is slightly deeper than the worktop to allow you to file it to a perfect fit.

2 Use contact adhesive to fix the strip in place. Sand the cut edge of the worktop, then apply a coat of adhesive and allow 10 minutes for it to go tacky. Then spread a second coat on the worktop edge and a coat on the edging strip and wait another 10 minutes.

3 Line up the bottom edge of the strip with the bottom of the worktop and glue the strip in place, butting it up to the wall at the back and allowing it to overhang slightly at the front. Use a hammer and a block of wood and tap along the edge to ensure a good fix.

4 Finish the top and front edges by filing them at an angle to a chamfer. File from the outer side towards the worktop, not in a see-saw motion, keeping the file at a constant angle.

Choosing a kitchen tap

Most taps work in the same way – turning the handle opens or closes a valve that fits into a valve seat. The valve – a rod and plate known as a jumper valve – is fitted with a washer that is replaced when it is worn and the tap drips.

High-neck taps The spout on an ordinary tap is about 22mm above its base, whereas the spout on a high-neck tap will be at least 95mm above its base. With a shallow sink this allows a bucket to be filled or large pans to be rinsed with ease. High neck taps are available with capstan, handwheel and lever handles. Most lever-handle taps have ceramic discs so require only a quarter turn of the handle.

MIXER TAPS

Two taps with a common spout are known as a mixer. The taps are linked either by a deck block (flat against the surface) or a pillar block (raised). Most kitchen mixers are monobloc types that fit into a single hole in the sink. Some mixers, however, need three holes – one for each handle and a centre hole for the spout.

Kitchen mixer The spout has separate channels for hot and cold water. This is because the kitchen cold tap is fed direct from the mains, and it is illegal to mix cold water from the mains and hot water from a storage cistern in one fitting. The spout usually swivels and should be able to reach both of the bowls in a double sink. Kitchen mixers are available with capstan, handwheel and lever handles. Some kitchen monobloc mixers include a hot-rinse spray and brush fed from the hot water pipe by a flexible hose, so that the spray can be lifted from its socket for use.

Choosing waste pipes and joints for a kitchen

Plastic waste pipes are made in 40mm and 50mm diameter for sinks and kitchen appliances, including washing machines and dishwashers. Pipes and fittings from different makers are not always interchangeable, so buy all the waste pipes and joints you need together. All waste water outlets must also be fitted with a trap (see page 69) to stop gas from the drain getting back into the room. Buy these at the same time to make sure that all your fittings are compatible.

uPVC (or PVC) For cold water overflow pipes from WC and storage cisterns. Joined by push-fit or ring-seal joints or by solvent welding. White, grey, brown, sometimes black. Sold in 3m and 4m lengths.

MuPVC (modified un-plasticised polyvinyl chloride) For hot waste from sinks, baths, washbasins and washing machines. Joined by push-fit or ring-seal joints, or by solvent welding (see below). Ring-seals for connection to main stack. Grey, white, sometimes black. Sold in 4m lengths.

Polypropylene For cold-water overflow pipes and hot waste from sinks, baths, washbasins and washing machines. Joined by push-fit or ring-seal joints only. White and black. Has slightly waxy surface. Sold in 3m and 4m lengths.

SPECIAL JOINTS FOR WASTE PIPES

Locking push-fit (ring-seal) joint
Polypropylene joint with screw-down retaining capnuts. The sealing ring is usually ready-fitted.

Push-fit (ring-seal) joint
Rigid polypropylene sleeve with a push-fit connection. Cannot be connected to any existing copper, steel or plastic system unless a locking ring fitting is interposed.

Solvent-weld joint
A plastic sleeve with a built-in pipe stop at each end. Used with PVC piping, which is secured in the sleeve by means of a strong adhesive, recommended by the joint manufacturer.

Expansion coupling
MuPVC joint designed for a solvent-weld joint at one end and a ring-seal joint at the other. Because solvent-weld joints do not allow for heat expansion, the coupling should be inserted every 1.8m in a long run of solvent-welded waste pipe.

Pipe strap
Straps or clips for supporting waste pipes are available in compatible sizes. For sloping pipes they should be fixed about every 500mm. The slope must be at least 20mm per 1m run. For vertical pipes, fix clips every 1.2m.

Stack connector
A clip-on polypropylene boss for fitting a new waste pipe into the stack, in which a hole has to be cut.

Joining pipes

To plumb in taps and appliances, you will need to make watertight joints.

Preparing the pipe ends

Before two pipe lengths of any material can be joined, the ends must be cut square and left smooth. You can cut plastic pipes with special shears or with a sharp craft knife.

Tools *Pipe cutter or hacksaw; half-round file. Possibly also vice or workbench.*

1 Cut the pipe ends square using a pipe cutter (above) or hacksaw. Holding the pipe in a vice helps to ensure a square cut.

2 Smooth off burrs inside the cut ends with the reamer on the pipe cutter. Use a file to smooth the end and the outside.

MIXED MEASUREMENTS

New plumbing fittings come in metric sizes, but if the plumbing in your house dates from before the mid 1970s, your pipework is in imperial sizes (½in, ¾in and 1in inner diameter). Modern copper pipe comes in outer diameters of 10mm, 15mm, 22mm and 28mm. Choose 15mm pipe to join to existing ½in pipework and 28mm for 1in pipework. You will need special connectors for joining 22mm pipe to ¾in pipework.

Making a compression joint

This is a strong and easy method of joining copper and plastic pipes. Compression joints produce a watertight seal by squeezing a metal ring, called an olive, between the pipe and the fitting. A capnut screwed onto the end of the joint puts the necessary pressure on the joint. Tightening the capnuts correctly is critical – the joint will leak if they are not tight enough or if they are over-tightened. Many flexible tap connectors and most washing machine and dishwasher isolation valves join to the main supply pipework with compression joints.

Tools *Two adjustable spanners (with jaw openings up to 38mm wide for fittings on 28mm piping).*

Materials *Compression fitting.*

1 Unscrew and remove one capnut from the fitting. If the olive has two sloping faces rather than a convex one, note which way round it is fitted, then remove it as well.

2 Take one pipe and slide the capnut over it, then the olive. Make sure the olive is the same way round as it was in the fitting if it has two sloping faces.

3 Push the pipe into one end of the fitting up to the internal pipe stop. Then slide the olive and nut up to the fitting and hand-tighten the capnut.

4 Hold the body of the fitting securely with one spanner while you give the capnut one and a quarter turns with the other. Do not overtighten it further. Fit pipes into other openings of the fitting in the same way.

Making a Speedfit joint

This is a simple method that can be used to join both copper and plastic pipes. The only tools needed are those used to cut and smooth the pipe ends.

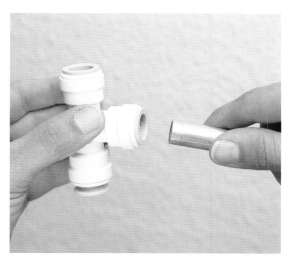

1 Take one of the pipe ends and push it into the fitting until it clicks into the toothed ring.

2 Fit piping into the other end(s) of the fitting in the same way.

Making a Hep$_2$O joint

This is a quick and simple method of joining polybutylene or copper pipes. To connect to old imperial-size pipework, you have to remove the capnut and O-ring seal and replace the seal with an adapter ring. Consult the manufacturer's fitting instructions.

Tools *Pencil; measuring tape.*

Materials *Silicone lubricant.*

1 Check that the cut pipe end is smooth, otherwise sharp edges could damage the O-ring seal in the fitting and cause the joint to leak.

2 For plastic piping, push the metal support sleeve into the pipe end.

3 Make a pencil mark on the pipe 25mm from the end. This marks the insertion depth of the pipe into the fitting.

4 Smear the end of the pipe with silicone lubricant as far as the pencil mark.

5 Push the pipe into the fitting up to the insertion mark. If it is not pushed fully home the pipe will blow out under pressure.

Fitting a waste pipe and trap

Before 1939, waste and overflow pipes for sinks, washbasins, baths and cisterns were made of lead or galvanised steel. After that, copper was used until about 1960. Since then plastic has been in general use.

Joints for joining waste pipes come in broadly the same configurations as those for joining supply pipes.

If you plan to fit a new pipe that has to be connected into a soil stack, get the approval of your local authority Building Control Officer.

Making a solvent-welded joint

Because solvent-welded joints are neat, they are suitable for exposed MuPVC pipework. However, they are permanent and should only be used where they will not need to be disturbed. Push-fit connections are used at traps, where the joint may need to be undone occasionally.

Tools *Hacksaw; half-round file; cloth.*

Materials *Solvent-weld cement; appropriate connector; appropriate pipe.*

1 Cut the pipes to the required length with a hacksaw, remove the burrs inside and out with a half-round file, and wipe thoroughly with a clean cloth.

2 Apply solvent-weld cement around the end of the pipe and push it into the joint.

3 Wipe off excess cement with the cloth and allow the joint to dry before moving on to the next joint.

Making a push-fit joint

Push-fit or ring-seal joints must be used to connect polypropylene waste pipes, which cannot be solvent-welded.

Tools *Hacksaw; sharp knife; clean rag; newspaper; adhesive tape; pencil.*

Materials *Push-fit joint; silicone grease.*

1 Wrap a sheet of newspaper round the pipe as a saw guide. Cut the pipe square with a hacksaw.

2 Use a sharp knife to remove fine shavings of polypropylene and any rough edges from the pipe, and wipe dust from inside the fitting and outside the pipe.

3 On a locking-ring connector, loosen the locking ring.

Sealing ring

Locking ring

4 Make sure that the sealing ring is properly in place, with any taper pointing inwards. If necessary, remove the nut to check.

5 Lubricate the end of the pipe with silicone grease.

6 Push the pipe into the socket as far as the stop – a slight inner ridge about 25mm from the end. This allows a gap of about 10mm at the pipe end for heat expansion.

Alternatively If there is no stop, push the pipe in as far as it will go, mark the insertion depth with a pencil, then withdraw the pipe 10mm to leave an expansion gap.

7 Tighten the locking ring.

Fitting a trap

Traps are either tubular or bottle-shaped (see Choosing a trap, right), and are made in suitable sizes to fit between a sink, bath or washbasin waste outlet and its waste pipe.

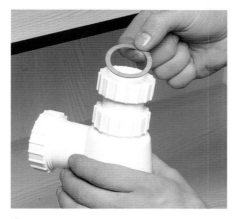

1 Check that the locking nut on the trap inlet is unscrewed and the rubber washer in position.

2 Push the trap inlet into the waste outlet and screw the nut onto the waste outlet thread.

3 Connect the trap outlet to the waste pipe with a push-fit joint.

CHOOSING A TRAP

There are different types of trap for different situations. There may also be different outlet types (vertical or horizontal) and seal depths. The seal – the depth of water held in the trap – is normally 38mm, but a trap with a deep seal of 75mm must, by law, be fitted to any appliance connected to a single-stack drainage pipe.

Tubular traps

A two-piece trap for a sink or basin, with an S (downpointing) outlet or a P (horizontal) outlet (right) and an adjustable inlet to allow an existing pipe to be linked to a new sink at a different height. Tubular traps are cleaned by unscrewing the part connected to the sink waste outlet.

Anti-siphon bottle trap

Designed to allow air to enter the trap and prevent the seal being lost. Use where there is an occasional heavy flow, or a long, steep pipe run.

Washing-machine trap

A tubular trap with a tall stand-pipe for the washing-machine waste hose, and an outlet to link to the waste pipe.

Plumbing in a washing machine or dishwasher

A washing machine or dishwasher is easy to install beside a kitchen sink, as the existing supply and waste pipes are conveniently positioned for fitting a drain kit and branch pipes for the machine.

Before you start When a washing machine or dishwasher is newly plumbed in, a double check valve (non-return valve) must be fitted to the hot and cold pipes supplying the hoses.

Drain kits will not fit every type of washing machine, so check in the manual or with the manufacturer before choosing one.

Tools *Hacksaw or pipe slice; half-round file; two adjustable spanners; medium-sized screwdriver; measuring tape; soft pencil; two spring-clip clothes pegs; spirit level. Possibly also shallow pan.*

Materials *About 600mm of 15mm copper piping; two washing machine stoptaps; two 15mm single check valves; two 15mm equal tee compression joints; one drain kit; one hose clip of the diameter of the drain hose.*

Connecting up the water

1 Turn off the water supply to the kitchen sink cold tap at the main stoptap.

2 Mark the cold supply pipe at a point convenient for connection to the machine. Make a second mark 20mm higher.

3 Cut through the pipe squarely with a hacksaw or pipe slice at the lowest point marked. A small amount of water will run

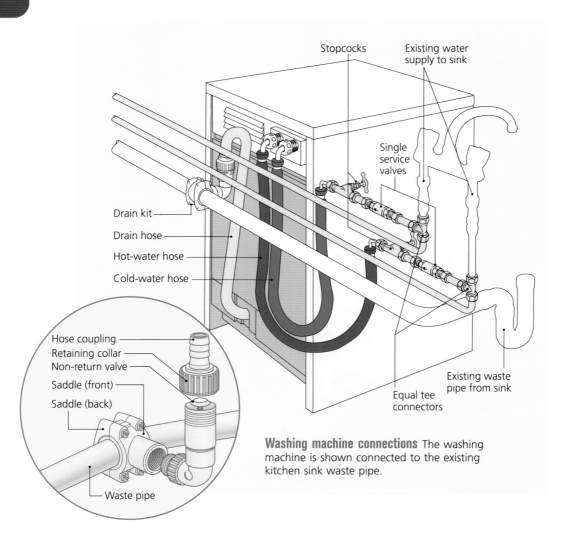

Washing machine connections The washing machine is shown connected to the existing kitchen sink waste pipe.

out as you cut the pipe. Cut at the second mark on the pipe and remove the section of pipe. File the pipe ends smooth.

4 Use spring-clip clothes pegs to stop the caps and olives slipping down the pipe. Fit a tee joint to the pipe with the branch outlet pointing towards the machine.

5 Cut a short length of pipe, fit it into the tee outlet and connect to the check valve, making sure that the valve's arrow mark points towards the machine.

6 Cut another length of pipe and fit it to the check valve outlet. It should be long enough to reach to the washing machine position.

7 Fit the other end of the pipe to the compression joint end of the machine stoptap. Connect the machine's cold-water hose to the stoptap.

8 Turn off the water supply to the hot tap over the kitchen sink. Cut the pipe and fit a tee joint, new pipe, check valve and stoptap as above. Connect the machine's hot-water hose to the stoptap and restore the hot and cold water supplies.

> ## EXPERT TIP
>
> Self-cutting taps can be fitted to the cold supply pipe to eliminate the need for turning off the water supply and cutting the pipework to fit a compression joint.

Fitting a self-cutting waste pipe

1 Unscrew the saddle from the rest of the drain kit.

2 Fit the saddle round the waste pipe. Choose a convenient place away from joints, and well beyond the trap.

3 Screw the cutting tool into the saddle until a hole has been cut in the waste pipe.

4 Remove the cutting tool and screw on the rest of the drain kit. It includes a non-return valve to prevent water from the sink flowing into the machine.

5 Slip a hose clip over the drain hose, push it into the spigot and tighten the clip. Now the machine is ready to use. Every two or three months, unscrew the plastic retaining collar and remove any fluff that may be clogging up the non-return valve. Be sure to tighten it fully afterwards.

🚫 Wiring in an electric cooker

Plan the cable route from the cooker control unit back to the consumer unit. It can be run beneath floorboards and chased into plaster before approaching the control unit vertically; or the cable can run in surface-mounted white plastic trunking at worktop or floor level.

Tools *Suitable tools for preparing the route; sharp knife; insulated screwdrivers; wire cutters and strippers; pliers.*

Materials *Cooker control unit with mounting box; cooker connection unit with mounting box (for a free-standing cooker); grommets; fixing screws and wallplugs; two-core-and-earth cable of the correct size; green-and-yellow plastic sleeving; cable clips; free-standing cooker or separate oven and hob; available fuse or MCB of the correct rating.*

Putting in the cables

There is no need to switch off at the mains until you are ready to connect the new circuit cable to the consumer unit.

1 Ask an electrician to check the earthing and bonding and remedy any defects. Prepare the route, leading it from near the consumer unit to the cooker control unit. From there lead it to the cooker connection unit behind a free-standing cooker, or to positions behind a separate oven and hob.

2 Fit the mounting box for the cooker control unit and, if you are installing a free-standing cooker, fit the mounting box for the connection unit. Remember to remove knock-outs from the mounting boxes for the cables to enter, and to fit grommets in the holes.

3 Fit lengths of cable along the route from the consumer unit to the control unit, and from the control unit to the connection unit or to positions behind the oven and hob. Do not feed the cable into the consumer unit but feed the other cable ends into the mounting boxes. Allow enough spare cable at the ends to reach all the terminals easily. Prepare the cable ends for connection, remembering to sleeve the earth conductors.

4 Repair the plaster and wait for it to dry. Replace any floorboards you have lifted.

Connecting at the control unit

1 Connect the cable from the consumer unit to the terminals of the control unit. Take the brown core to the terminal marked L and In. Screw the blue core into that marked N and In. Screw the green-and-yellow-sleeved earth core into the nearer of the terminals marked E or ⏚.

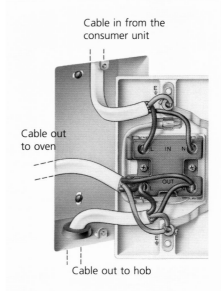

Cable in from the consumer unit

Cable out to oven

Cable out to hob

Connecting at the control unit
Two cables lead to a separate oven and hob. Only one goes to a free-standing cooker or to the oven and hob if they are to one side of the control unit.

2 Connect the cable leading out to the connection unit or oven and hob into the terminals behind the control unit plate. Take the brown core to the terminal marked L and Out, and the blue core to the terminal marked N and Out. Connect the green-and-yellow-sleeved earth core to the nearer of the terminals marked E or ⏚.

If you are leading separate cables to an oven and hob, there will be two outgoing sets of cores. Match the cores in pairs – brown with brown, blue with blue and green-and-yellow with green-and-yellow. Insert the pairs of cores into the correct terminals and screw them in place.

Connecting a free-standing cooker at the connection unit

1 Remove the screws holding the cover to the metal frame. Then unscrew and remove the cable clamp at the bottom of the frame.

Wiring at the connection unit

Cable from control unit

Cable clamp

Cable to free-standing cooker

2 Pair the cable cores from the control unit and to the cooker – brown with brown, blue with blue, and green-and-yellow with green-and-yellow. Screw the pairs into the terminal block on the frame – brown to L, blue to N and green-and-yellow to E or ⏚.

3 Screw the frame to the mounting box and screw on the cable clamp.

4 Screw the cover of the connection unit in place.

Connecting to a free-standing cooker

1 Remove the metal plate covering the terminals on the back of the cooker. Release the cable clamp.

2 Connect the supply cable cores to their terminals – brown to L and blue to N. Usually the cores have to be bent round a pillar and held down with brass washers

and nuts. Make sure enough insulation has been removed for the bare wire to wind round the pillars. Connect the green-and-yellow sleeved earth core to E or ⏚.

3 Screw the clamp over the cable. Screw the plate back over the terminals.

Connecting to the consumer unit

1 Turn off the main switch at the consumer unit and take out the fuse carrier or switch off the MCB for the cooker circuit. Make sure the control unit and all cooker controls are off.

2 Remove the screws of the consumer unit cover and take it off.

3 Drill through the frame of the consumer unit if it is wooden, or knock out an entry hole and fit a grommet if it is a metal or plastic one. Feed in the cable. Make sure that you have removed enough outer sheath for the cores to reach the terminals.

4 Screw the blue core into a spare terminal at the neutral terminal block and screw the brown core into the terminal on the spare fuseway or MCB.

5 Screw the green-and-yellow sleeved earth core into a spare terminal at the earth terminal block.

6 Replace the circuit fuse or switch on the MCB.

7 Screw on the cover of the consumer unit and turn the main switch back on.

Understanding an electric cooker circuit

An electric cooker uses so much electricity that it must have its own circuit. If it shared a circuit with other appliances the circuit would frequently be overloaded.

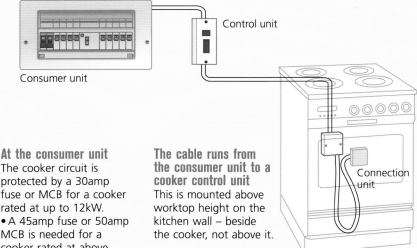

Consumer unit

Control unit

Connection unit

Free standing cooker

At the consumer unit
The cooker circuit is protected by a 30amp fuse or MCB for a cooker rated at up to 12kW.
• A 45amp fuse or 50amp MCB is needed for a cooker rated at above 12kW.
• A separate oven and hob operating on the same circuit may have a higher rating than 12kW.

The cable runs from the consumer unit to a cooker control unit
This is mounted above worktop height on the kitchen wall – beside the cooker, not above it.

From the control unit to the cooker
The cable enters the appliance and is wired into its terminal block.
• The size of two-core-and-earth cable needed depends on both the wattage of the cooker and the length of the cable run. For a circuit with a 30-amp fuse or MCB, use 6mm² cable if the total length of the cable run is up to 20m, and use 10mm² cable if the total length of the cable run is between 20m and 30m.
• For a circuit with a 45-amp fuse or 50-amp MCB, use 10mm² cable for a run of up to 10m, and 16mm² cable for a run of between 11m and 22m.

The cooker control unit
This is a double-pole switch that disconnects both the live and neutral conductors. The unit may have a neon light that glows when the unit is switched on.

Many older units included a 13amp socket outlet, but these are best avoided because they take too long to disconnect if an appliance plugged into the outlet develops an earth fault. If the control unit includes a socket outlet, a 30amp fuse or MCB will still be suitable for a cooker rated at up to 10kW.

For a free-standing cooker
A second length of cable runs from the control unit to a cooker connection unit fitted on the wall about 600mm above floor level behind the cooker. A 2m length of cable runs from the connection unit to the cooker, so that the cooker can be drawn away from the wall when necessary. Use the same size of cable for this as for the rest of the circuit.

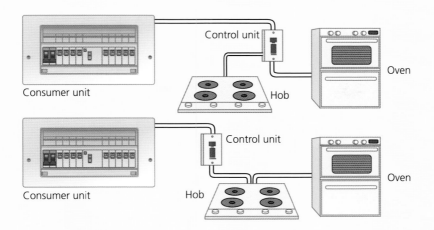

Consumer unit — Control unit — Oven — Hob

Consumer unit — Control unit — Oven — Hob

For a separate oven and hob These can be connected to one cooker control unit provided that neither the hob nor the oven is more than 2m away from the control unit.
• You can make the connection by running two cables from the control unit, one to the oven and the other to the hob.
• Alternatively, you can run one length of cable from the control unit to one part of the cooker and a second length of cable from there to the second part of the cooker.
• No connection units are needed on the wall behind a separate oven and hob because they are permanently built in.

CONNECTING A SEPARATE OVEN AND HOB

If you have led two cables from the control unit, one each for the oven and hob, connect each cable in the same way as a free-standing cooker (page 73) and secure under the clamp.

Alternatively, if you have led one cable from the cooker control unit to the first component, you will have two cables to connect and clamp there – one from the control unit and one to the second component.

Match the cores – brown with brown, blue with blue, and green-and-yellow with green-and-yellow. Connect them to the terminals – brown to L, blue to N, and green-and-yellow to E or ⏚.

Connect the ongoing cable to the second component as for a free-standing cooker.

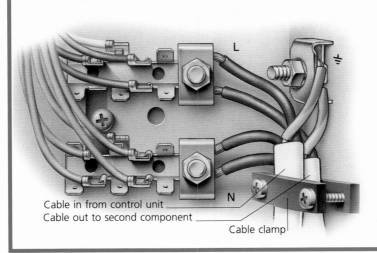

Cable in from control unit
Cable out to second component
Cable clamp

Fitting low-voltage recessed spotlights

Brilliant, low-voltage lights are ideal for kitchens. Because they are small, it is possible to site lights directly above where they are needed, thus avoiding the shadows and dark areas that can arise with more traditional centrally mounted lighting.

These instructions that follow relate to a typical installation of ceiling-mounted recessed lights. Not all lights are identical, so be sure to read and understand the installation instructions that come with your particular lights, as there may be differences from those described here. The manufacturer's instructions will outline any restrictions on siting the lights and transformer.

Tools *Pencil; padsaw, or power drill with holesaw attachment, probably 57mm in diameter; compasses; insulated screwdriver; wire cutters and strippers.*

Materials *Low-voltage lights with individual transformers; two-core-and-earth cable; junction boxes.*

Before you start Although low-voltage lighting is very safe, the transformers connect to the 230-volt mains circuit and must be treated accordingly.

1 Decide on where you want to site the lights and draw circles on the ceiling the

HELPFUL TIP

Use a stud finder to check the positions of ceiling joists in the area that you wish to place the lights and mark these with a pencil. Ideally, lights should be placed centrally between the joists. Bear in mind that if you position most of the lights between the same two joists, you will have less trouble running cables than if you place them between different joists, as you will not need to drill through joists for the cables.

same diameter as the light fittings. Then use a holesaw of this diameter – usually 57mm – fitted to a power drill, to cut perfect holes fast and accurately.

Alternatively Drill a hole inside each circle large enough to admit a padsaw blade and cut the holes by hand.

2 Switch off the power at the mains and remove the fuse or switch off the MCB protecting the circuit you are working on. Run the cable from the original light fitting to the nearest new light position. Terminate it at a junction box together with a new length of 1mm² two-core-and-earth cable. Run the new cable to the next light in the sequence until each hole has wiring to it and a junction box to connect into. You will probably need to do this from above, by lifting the floorboards, unless you have removed the kitchen ceiling as part of more major renovations. Use a power drill with a 12mm wood bit if you have to make cable holes through any joists.

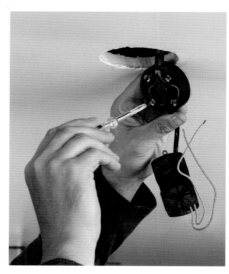

3 At each location, wire in the transformer supply lead to the junction box.

4 Connect each light to its transformer, using the plastic strip connectors supplied. Then push each transformer up into the ceiling void, leaving the bulb connectors hanging down.

5 Push the fire hoods up into the ceiling void, taking care not to push the bulb connectors with them.

SAFETY WARNING

Each recessed spotlight should be fitted within a smoke hood. This sits in the ceiling void above each

spotlight and prevents smoke from the kitchen rising through gaps in the ceiling and floorboards to the upper floors, in the event of a fire.

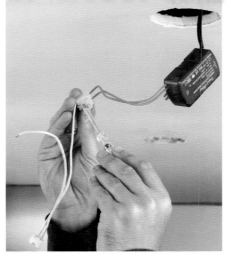

6 Insert the light fittings into the holes until you hear them click: as you push the light up, the shorter arms on the clips force the longer arms to flatten against the upper surface of the ceiling.

7 Fit a halogen bulb into each light fitting. Push the bulbs into place and snap on the metal ring clip to hold them. Turn on the power at the main switch to check the operation of the lights. If you need to change a bulb at a later date, gently squeeze the ends of the metal ring clip together so you can remove it and take out the bulb. Be sure to replace it with one of the same wattage.

Fitting an under-cupboard lighting kit

The simplest way to illuminate your worktops is with a chain of linked fluorescent strip lights that are plugged in to an electric socket.

This job does not involve any mains wiring, so can be done without notifying the Building Control Officer and without professional certification. Once the lights are in position, you simply plug the master light (the first in the run) into a nearby mains socket, which powers all the lights. Each light has its own rocker switch. Make sure the plug has a 3amp (red) fuse, not a 13amp (brown) one.

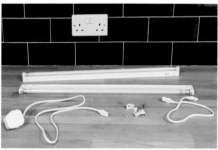

The striplights are sold in kit form – together with fixing screws, cable clips and two-core connecting flexes that simply plug in to link the run of lights together.

1 Allow one fitting for every 500mm of worktop. Lay the kit out along the worktop to plan exactly where you will fit the lights, making sure that there is a socket within reach of the master light (the one with a flex and plug).

2 Position the clips and screw them into the underside of the wall units. Do not fix the lights closer than 50mm from the wall or they may overheat. They will be best disguised by the lighting pelmet if they are near the front edge of the cupboards.

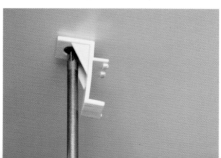

3 Plug in the connecting cables to link all the lights together. Each linking cable has a plug at one end and a socket at the other, so it will be obvious how to fit them.

4 Lift the lights into position and secure them in their clips. Neaten any excess cable by pinning it to the underside of the cupboards using plastic cable clips.

5 Plug in and switch on at the mains socket, and test each light using its rocker switch.

Wiring in under-cupboard lights

Low-voltage spotlights and striplights can be wired into the mains lighting circuit and can be operated from a single main switch.

Spotlight kits are often sold with a single transformer to run more than one light, depending on the wattage of the bulbs. A 100W transformer will power 5 x 20W bulbs, for example. These transformers have multiple outlet sockets, but if you need to run more lights than there are sockets you can wire one outlet to a junction box.

1 Turn off the lighting circuit at the consumer unit before you start work.

2 Prepare a chase for the cable and run 1mm² two-core-and-earth cable from the main light switch to a convenient point in the wall either above or below a wall cupboard, where you will be able to mount the transformer.

3 If you position the transformer on top of a cupboard, drill a hole in the base of the cupboards at each light position and, one at a time, feed a length of stiff wire or a flexible rod up from the worktop to the top of the cupboard. Each light will have a length of cable to run from the light to the transformer. Tape this securely to the worktop end of your wire or rod and pull it through to the transformer position.

4 Wire the light cables into the transformer. If you are mounting the transformer under the cupboards, this can be done at worktop level.

5 Fix each light in turn (or their clips, if they have them) to the base of the cupboards. The light surrounds and brackets are one unit in this case.

6 Clip the bulbs into position or fix the lights to their clips, as appropriate.

7 Terminate the connections at the light switch then turn the power back on at the consumer unit and test the lights.

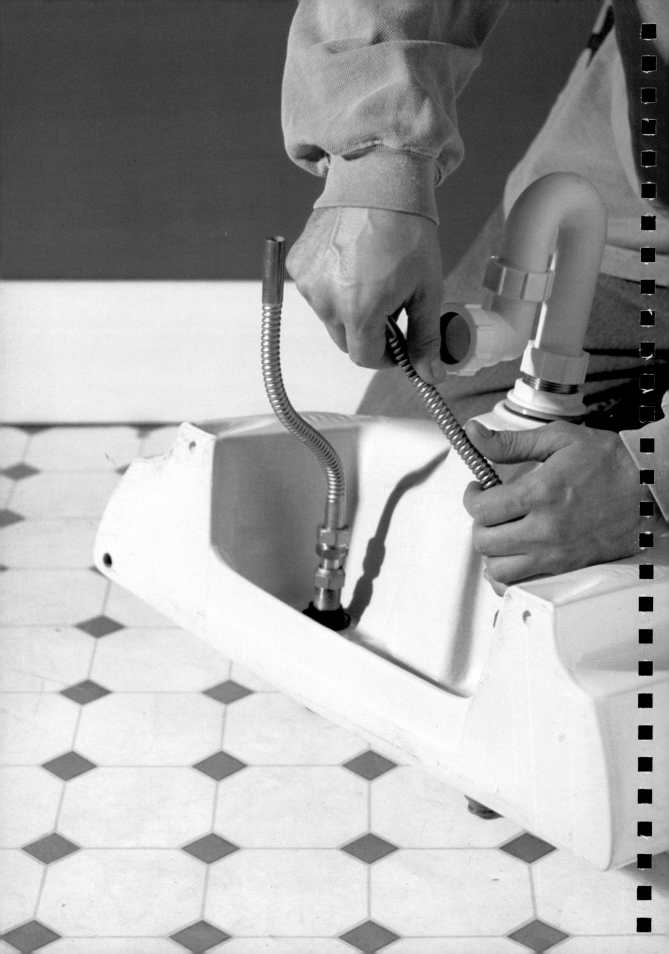

Fitting a new bathroom

Planning a new bathroom

Most bathroom fittings come in a range of standard sizes. To use them comfortably, you need to allow a minimum amount of space around each one.

The minimum you are likely to want to fit into your bathroom is a bath, WC and basin. You may also wish to include a separate shower cubicle, perhaps a bidet or a second basin. The simplest plan when replacing your bathroom suite is to replace like for like, fitting each new item in the same position as the original. However, to make the best use of the space you have it may make sense to rearrange the bathroom into a new design. Follow the advice given here to make sure that you allow enough room to use and move around the room comfortably.

Standard sizes

Always check the sizes of the fittings you are planning to buy. Most come in a range of standard sizes – do not assume that they will be the same size as the pieces in your existing suite. Slimline WC cisterns, corner basins, corner shower trays and cubicles and even corner WCs are available and can be useful options for a very small space.
• **Baths** Standard rectangular baths are 1700mm x 750mm. They are also available in 1600 and 1800mm lengths and narrower and broader widths. Corner baths may be a true quadrant, with two straight sides of 1500mm, or offset, measuring 1500mm x 1000mm. Look out for shower baths that are wider at one end and 'studio' baths that taper towards one end. Free-standing baths are generally wider and require more space around them to make the most of their effect.
• **Showers** Trays and shower enclosures are available in a wide range of shapes and sizes. A standard 700mm square cubicle is the most common, but larger squares (up to 900mm), rectangles up to 1200mm long and quadrants and pentangles, like a square with the corner cut off are also available.
• **WCs** Free-standing WCs are between 350mm and around 500mm wide. Built-in options have the cistern concealed in a fitted unit, or you can house it in a marine plywood structure that is then tiled to match the rest of the room.

Position a light and mirror above the basin. Many bathroom lights also incorporate a shaver socket, or you may choose an integrated light and mirror. Mirror-fronted medicine cabinets (lockable if there are children in the house) are a good use of space.

Allow an arc with a radius of 600mm around the door opening if the door opens into the room. Make sure that you will be able to move around the room when the door is open.

To stand comfortably at a basin, you will need a radius 700mm wide, measured from the rim of the basin.

• **Basins** You can find a basin to fit whatever space you have, from tiny cloakroom basins just large enough for washing your hands to wide 'design statement' modern washstand options or stylish bowls that will sit on the countertop of a fitted unit.

Make sure that all bathroom light fittings conform with Building Regulations and have the appropriate zone rating for their position in the room (see page s 20–21).

Try to leave a clearance of at least 1m in front of the opening side of a shower cubicle to allow room for you to step in and out and to dry yourself. If the door of the shower cubicle opens outwards, increase this to 1.5m.

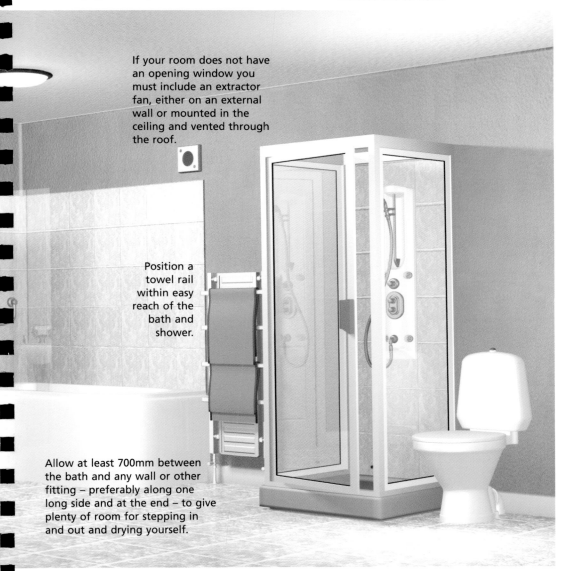

If your room does not have an opening window you must include an extractor fan, either on an external wall or mounted in the ceiling and vented through the roof.

Position a towel rail within easy reach of the bath and shower.

Allow at least 700mm between the bath and any wall or other fitting – preferably along one long side and at the end – to give plenty of room for stepping in and out and drying yourself.

'Shower baths' have a wider bulge and steeper or vertical internal sides at the tap end to make a comfortable space for showering. If you choose a glass shower screen, make sure that you have room for it to open so that you can reach the taps and shower controls. Concertina screens are a useful option in a small space.

Centre a WC in a gap at least 600mm wide, but preferably wider if you can and allow 600mm in front of the rim. Allow the same space around a bidet, plus a little extra leg room on each side. A WC that is squeezed into a narrow space will be difficult to clean around.

Choosing a style of bathroom

With today's exciting ranges of fittings, tiles, flooring materials and lighting, there is no excuse for a dull bathroom. Would a bright modern style suit your family, or do you lean towards a period look? Perhaps the idea of a wet room tempts you – but think about the needs of the whole family before choosing this option.

A basic bathroom suite includes basin, bath and WC. Most ranges offer matching bidets, too. The majority of new bathroom fittings are white or off white, but you can introduce any colour you like with paint, tiles and accessories.

Traditional bathrooms Ranges include Victorian, Edwardian, Georgian – even Gothic. They may offer a roll-top cast iron bath on feet, a high level WC, a pedestal basin and decorative brass or chrome accessories. And when stylishly executed, as in this pure white bathroom (below), the look is anything but old fashioned.

Modern bathrooms The clean lines of contemporary bathrooms suggest space and sophistication. Consider wall-hung

sanitary ware, counter top vessel basins and sleek storage units to give a minimalist feel (above). Designer taps can be mounted on the basin or bath or emerge straight from the wall, which also conceals the toilet cistern and pipework. This style works well with walk-in showers and wet rooms.

Small bathrooms Even small bathrooms can exude style. Space-saving designs make use of corner or wall-hung sanitary ware, shower baths, light neutral colours and good quality lighting. Clever placing of mirrors can give an illusion of space.

Bath or shower? If you have room for a bath, include one. You may be a 'shower person' but other family members – or the future occupants of your house – may like nothing better than a soak at the end of the day. Ideally, fit both. If there is room for a separate cubicle, then include one. If not, a shower unit can be fitted at one end of the bath, with glass screens or curtains to contain the water (facing page). The two most important considerations when choosing a shower are thermostatic control and adequate flow rate: seek advice from a plumber. Depending on your water system, pumps and power showers can transform a trickle into an invigorating shower.

Wet room The latest vogue in bathroom design is the wet room (right). This is a totally waterproof room – or part of a room – in which the floor is the shower tray and the shower waste outlet is a drain set into the floor. Most wet rooms are fully tiled in stone or ceramic tiles, and wall-hung sanitary ware is usually fitted.

Cleaning is a simple matter of mopping walls and floors with a squeegee and hosing down.

Wet rooms are expensive to install, however, as they first have to be 'tanked' (in other words, fully sealed and waterproofed), preferably by a professional.

Showers Showers range from bath tap attachments (right), useful for rinsing hair, to luxurious walk-in cubicles complete with huge overhead 'rain-shower' roses and body jets. Choose the largest size cubicle that you can accommodate, but be sure to allow enough room to get in and out of the shower easily. Modern designs mean that you don't necessarily need a lot of space for a shower: trays vary in size, from compact corner designs (above) to spacious walk-in models. If space is limited, consider sliding, inward-opening or bi-fold doors.

Shower trays Acrylic trays are cheap but best avoided because, as the trays flex, they tend to leak. The best option is a ceramic stone tray – heavy, solid and secure.

Bathroom storage

Your need for bathroom storage depends largely on the size of your household. There are several storage solutions for bathrooms.

Towel rail A heated towel rail that doubles as a bathroom radiator is both practical and glamorous (left). Choose a dual fuel rail that links into the central heating system, but which can be electrically heated when the central heating is switched off.

Open shelves These are readily accessible for items you use every day – toothpaste, shaving gel and so forth. Wire shelving inside a shower enclosure means you can store shampoos and shower gels within reach; you'll also want a shelf – or handy window sill – beside the bath.

Concealed storage One neat solution is an under-basin drawer (below). A cleverly designed cut-out allows space for the trap. A drawer for bathroom cleaning products can also be fitted into the panelling at one end of a bath.

A **lockable medicine cupboard** is vital if you have young children. Slimline mirrored bathroom cabinets are available with integral lighting and shaver socket (which can also be used to charge an electric toothbrush).

Dry cupboard Somewhere dry and warm – ideally an airing cupboard – is needed for storing clean towels. This does not necessarily have to be in the bathroom.

Laundry bin You may want a bin for used towels and dirty clothes. Look for one that doubles up as a seat to save space.

Toy storage Store kids' rubber ducks in a specially designed mesh bag, which fixes to the side of the bath or to smooth tiles with suction cups, and allows toys to drip dry.

Choosing lighting, heating and ventilation

Nothing beats natural light, and a bathroom window is a great asset both for light and ventilation. But the importance of artificial lighting in the bathroom – a room often used when it's dark outside – is easily underestimated.

The choice of lighting can determine the ambiance of a bathroom. Poor lighting feels dull and dingy; excessively bright lights can look cold and clinical. The right lighting feels warm, bright and welcoming. A family bathroom needs bright main lighting to illuminate skiddy patches of water on the floor. If you have small children, make sure they can reach the pull cord for night visits to the toilet. In an adult-only household, you can have fun with subtle or romantic lighting, keeping the bright lights for areas such as the shaving mirror above the basin.

The bathroom mirror You need to be able to see yourself properly, for example when shaving, putting in contact lenses or applying make-up. Provide efficient illumination where it is needed by fitting a diffused glass light on either side of the mirror, a fluorescent strip over it, or a halogen downlight in the ceiling immediately above the mirror (below). Or make a design statement with a mirror and light combined, such as this striking oval example (right).

General lighting The bulk of the bathroom is best illuminated by recessed halogen downlights, which cast a refreshing light, and don't gather dust. Alternatively, fit a high-output flush ceiling light in a style that coordinates with the design of your room.

Directional spot lights Lamps with trailing flexes are not permitted in bathrooms, but you can create subtle effects with ceiling mounted directional spot lights directed at pictures or ornaments – not at the bath.

Showers Lights designed specifically for showers are available. To meet safety standards, these must be carefully fitted according to manufacturers' instructions.

Regulations New regulations describe bathrooms in terms of 'zones', related to their proximity to water. Care must be taken to choose lighting appropriate to the relevant zone (see pages 20–21).

Extractor fans Always install an extractor fan – ideally one that comes on with the light and remains on for a few minutes once the light has been switched off.

Underfloor heating This form of heating is perfect in bathrooms, especially when combined with a heated towel rail (page 85). It is inexpensive to install and economical to run, using as much electricity as a standard light bulb per square metre. The most straightforward type to lay comes in the form of matting. The heating cable (the element) snakes back and forth through a cut-to-fit mesh mat, which is stuck to the bathroom floor. The cable must start and finish at the same point for connection to an electrical outlet. Heat output is thermostatically controlled with a special regulator. Your chosen flooring finish – stone or ceramic tiles are the best option – is simply laid on top. This kind of heating is suitable for use in wet rooms.

SUNLIGHT PIPES

An ingenious and environmentally sound way to provide light and air to an internal, windowless bathroom or shower room is the sunlight pipe. Known as Sola-vent, the system consists of a sun pipe, a solar-powered fan and two low voltage 50W halogen lights, all housed in one unit. The unit combines solar powered ventilation and natural daylight from the rooftop and is effective even under overcast skies. A light catching prism on the roof, and a sun pipe with a highly reflective lining, bring natural light into the room during daylight hours. A motion sensor automatically switches on an extractor fan when someone goes into the bathroom, so there is no need for a manual switch. The low maintenance fan unit has been designed to be as quiet and unintrusive as possible. The unit complies with current Building Regulations. (For more information, visit www.sunpipe.co.uk)

Planning a shower

Water pressure at the shower head is important. If it is too low, the flow of water from the rose will be weak.

For a mixer supplied from the household's stored hot and cold supplies, the bottom of the cold-water cistern needs to be at least 900mm – and preferably 1.5m – above the showerhead for pressure to be adequate.

For an instantaneous shower supplied direct from the mains, the pressure requirement varies according to the model, but in most homes it is unlikely to be too low, unless, perhaps, you live on the top floor of a block of flats, or in an old house converted into flats. Contact your local water company if in doubt.

Water supply and drainage

Little or no pipework is involved in installing a shower over a bath, but supply and drainage routes must be worked out for a shower in a separate cubicle. The drainage is often more difficult to arrange than the water supply to the shower, and you may need to get approval from your local authority Building Control Officer.

Use 15mm diameter supply pipes. To minimise loss of pressure, pipe runs to the shower should be as short and straight as possible. Avoid using elbow joints at corners – instead, bend pipes if possible to minimise resistance to flow. When routing a pipe, ensure that fixings will not interfere with electric cables or gas pipes.

Showers that do involve extra pipework over a bath are instantaneous electric showers and mixer types. For an instantaneous shower you need a cold supply pipe taken direct from the rising main; for a mixer shower, you need hot and cold supply pipes.

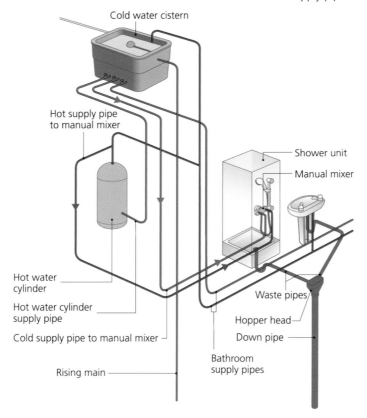

Cold water cistern

Hot supply pipe to manual mixer

Shower unit

Manual mixer

Hot water cylinder

Hot water cylinder supply pipe

Waste pipes

Cold supply pipe to manual mixer

Hopper head

Down pipe

Rising main

Bathroom supply pipes

Pipework for a shower mixer For a manual mixer, take the cold supply pipe direct from the cold water cistern to avoid risk of scalding when other cold taps are turned on. Take the hot supply from the hot water cylinder distribution pipe – tee in above cylinder height. For a thermostatic mixer, which has a temperature stabiliser, you can connect to bathroom supply pipes.

Shower mixers If you are installing a manual mixer over a bath or in a cubicle, you must take the cold supply direct from the storage cistern. Taking the supply from a branch pipe supplying other taps or cisterns is unsafe because when the other fitting is in use, the cold supply to the shower could be reduced so much that the shower becomes scalding.

Hot water for the mixer can be taken from a branch pipe, because there is no danger if the hot supply to the shower is reduced – though it can give you a nasty chilly spray. If you take the hot supply from the cylinder distribution pipe, make the connection at a point above the height of the cylinder top.

With a thermostatic shower mixer, however, both hot and cold water can be taken from the branch pipes, as the water temperature is automatically controlled.

Achieving adequate pressure

If you do not have sufficient water pressure to supply a shower at the required position, there are two ways to increase it: you can either raise the height of the cistern or have a booster pump installed.

Raising the cistern The cold water cistern can be raised by fitting a strong wooden platform beneath it, constructed from timber struts and blockboard. You will also have to lengthen the rising main to reach the cistern, as well as the distribution pipes from the cistern.

Booster pumps These incorporate an electric motor and must be wired into the power supply. There are two main types. A single pump is fitted between the mixer control and the spray and boosts the mixed supply to the spray. A dual pump is fitted to the supply pipes and boosts the hot and cold supplies separately before they reach the mixer. Depending on the model, a booster pump will provide sufficient pressure with as little as 150mm height difference between the water level in the cistern and the spray head.

Most dual pumps need to be at least 300mm below the cold tank, but some will provide sufficient pressure to a showerhead sited higher than the cold water storage cistern, which allows a shower to be installed in an attic.

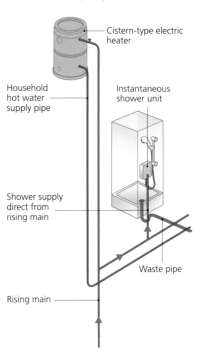

Cistern-type electric heater

Household hot water supply pipe

Instantaneous shower unit

Shower supply direct from rising main

Waste pipe

Rising main

Pipework for an instantaneous shower
Here, only a cold supply, direct from the rising main, is needed. This is useful where there is no cold water storage cistern, as mains cold water and stored hot water cannot, by law, be mixed in one fitting.

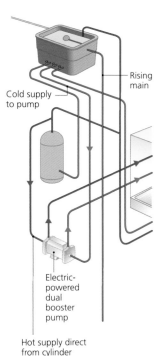

Rising main

Cold supply to pump

Electric-powered dual booster pump

Hot supply direct from cylinder

Boosting water pressure with a dual pump
This boosts hot and cold water supplies separately. Some types of pump have a hot supply pipe direct from the cylinder casing, some from the vent pipe. A dual booster pump should be fitted by a plumber.

Choosing a shower

The type of shower that can be installed depends in part on your household water system. Where hot and cold water are both supplied from storage tanks at equal pressure (see A typical indirect (two circuit) system, page 14), a mixer shower is the most economical option. Many showers are designed to cope with differing water pressures, such as stored hot water and cold mains water. If you connect mains water to a shower, you must fit a double seal check valve on the mains supply pipe to prevent back siphonage. Some showers come with built-in check valves. Specially designed systems are required when hot water is to be supplied from the mains via a multipoint heater or combination boiler: check the installation requirements with the shower manufacturer.

Bath/shower mixer A shower spray combined with a bath mixer tap provides a shower for little more than the cost of the bath taps, and no extra plumbing is involved. The temperature is controlled through the bath taps, which may not be convenient, and will be affected by water being drawn off elsewhere in the home.

Power shower An all-in-one shower which incorporates a powerful electric pump that boosts the rate that hot and cold water are supplied to the shower head from the storage cistern and the hot water cylinder. A power shower is unsuitable where water is supplied from a combination boiler under mains pressure. Removing waste water from a power shower fast enough can be a problem. The shower tray must cope with around 27 litres a minute, so it is probably worth fitting a 50mm waste pipe.

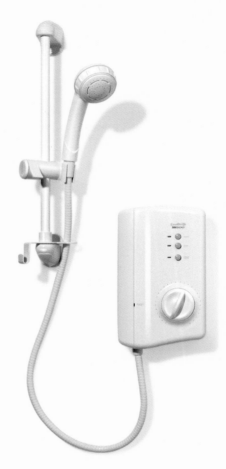

SAFETY WARNING

A showerhead on a hose must be fed through a retaining ring on the wall of the shower. This prevents the showerhead hanging in standing water in the bath or shower tray beneath and avoids potential contamination of the mains supply.

WETROOMS

A wetroom consists of a WC, basin and shower area. No shower tray or enclosure is fitted and water drains through a central drain set in a sloping floor, so the whole room must be waterproofed. This is not a DIY job. Wetrooms may have a powerful thermostatic mixer shower and body jets or a shower tower.

Instantaneous electric shower A wall unit plumbed in to a mains cold water supply, and heated by an electric element. The controls allow either less water at a higher temperature or more at a lower temperature, so the spray is weaker in winter when mains water is colder. Some models have a winter/summer setting. Designs fitted with a temperature stabiliser cannot run too hot or be affected by other taps in use. The unit must be wired to an electric power supply meeting Wiring Regulations requirements. This type of shower can be installed where a mixer would be illegal. Where mains water pressure is too low, a tank-fed pumped electric shower is available.

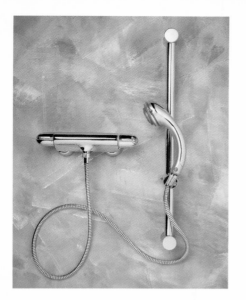

Manual and thermostatic mixers (above)
These are wall units with hot and cold water supplies linked to a single valve. In a manual mixer, temperature and volume are controlled by one dial or separately. Thermostatic mixers are more expensive. Their temperature control has a built-in stabiliser so water cannot run too hot or too cold. Computerised models have a control panel to programme temperature and flow rate and can store the data for each user. Provided water is not supplied from a combination boiler under mains pressure, this type of shower can be linked to a pump to give power shower performance.

SHOWER FITTINGS

Spray roses Showerheads may be fixed or part of a handset on a flexible hose. The simplest have a single spray; multi-spray showerheads offer a choice of spray patterns selected by rotating the outer ring on the rose. Large diameter single spray showerheads offering a rain-style shower are also available.

Shower trays GRP-reinforced acrylic trays are light to handle and not easily damaged. A reconstituted stone or resin shower tray is heavy, stable and durable, but the floor must be level before it is installed. Shower trays come in sizes from 700mm square and are usually 110–185mm high; low level 35mm trays are available for 'walk-in' showers. Quarter circle and pentangle trays help to save space.

Shower tower (below) A wall unit that incorporates a thermostatic mixer shower with a number of adjustable body jets. Tower units also have a fixed showerhead and a hand-held spray, and may be designed to fit into a corner or on a flat wall. Some can be installed over a bath while others are made for cubicles or wet rooms. Most require a minimum ceiling height of 2.2m. A pump is usually needed to boost water pressure.

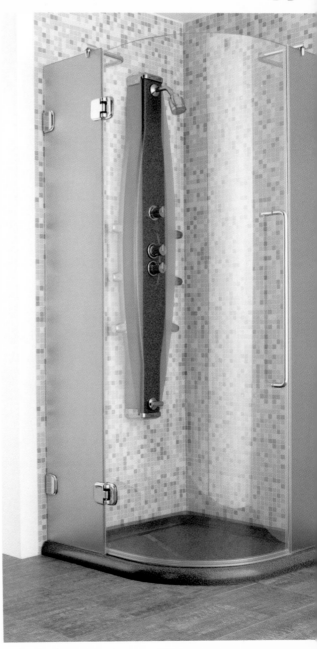

Choosing bathroom taps and traps

Your choice of tap can set the style for your bathroom, but there are some practical considerations, too.

MIXER TAPS

Two taps with a common spout are known as a mixer. The taps are linked either by a deck block (flat against the surface) or a pillar block (raised). Most mixers are two-hole types that fit into a standard two-hole-sink or bath: one for the hot tap and one for the cold. Some mixers, however, need three holes (a centre hole for the spout and a hole for each handle) and some (monobloc types) only one.

Bath/shower mixer
Bath/shower mixer taps have a control knob that diverts the water flow from the spout to the shower handset. It will not provide a forceful spray but is a convenient addition to a bath.

Bath or basin mixer Hot and cold water merge within the mixer body, as both taps are usually fed from a cistern. It is illegal to fit this type of mixer on a fitting where cold water is supplied from the rising main and hot water comes from a cylinder. This is because, if mains pressure alters, differences in pressure might result in stored water being sucked back into the mains, and create the possible risk of contaminating drinking water supplies.

Pillar tap The type still often used in bathrooms, with a vertical inlet that fits through a hole in the sanitaryware. The conventional tap has a bell-shaped cover – generally known as an easy-clean cover – and a capstan (cross-top) handle.

TRAPS FOR BATHROOM FITTINGS

There are different types of trap for different situations. The seal – or depth of water maintained in the trap – is normally 38mm, but a trap with a deep seal of 75mm must, by law, be fitted to any appliance connected to a single-stack drainage pipe. This guards against the seal being destroyed by an outflow of water, allowing foul gas from the stack to enter the house.

Overflow assembly

Cleaning eye

Bath trap with cleaning eye and overflow pipe
A cleaning eye can be unscrewed to clear a blockage and is useful where access is difficult. A flexible overflow pipe can be connected to a side or rear inlet on some bath traps.

Standard bottle trap Use only for washbasins, which usually have a small outflow. Most have a P outlet, but an S converter may be available. Some have a telescopic tube to adjust to different heights.

Planning the job

Living without a working bathroom is very inconvenient, so, unless you have a second bathroom in the house, plan your work carefully to minimise the disruption.

You may be able to replace your bathroom fittings one by one, over the course of several days or weekends if you are not changing their position. Even so, if you are planning to tile the whole floor you will need to do this in one sitting, in an empty room. In small rooms you may not be able to manoeuvre the old bath out or the new bath into the room until you have taken out the WC and basin. Here are some points to consider when planning your work to make sure that the project runs as smoothly as possible.

Check the connections Check before you start whether water supply and drainage pipes will need to be modified. Even if you are putting fittings back in the same place do not assume that the new ones are the same size as the old, nor that the pipes will all connect in the same place. You can use flexible tap connectors to accommodate slight differences in position.

Drainage If you will be re-routeing waste pipes and making new connections into an existing soil stack contact your local Building Control Department about making a Building Notice application.

Fixing to stud walls Consider whether you will need to reinforce any stud walls or floors. If you plan to fit a wall-hung basin or WC to a stud wall, the plasterboard will not be strong enough to hold it. You will need to cut away the plasterboard and fit an extra nogging or a support frame to bear the weight. Similarly, you may need to strengthen a floor to support a cast iron bath – ask your bath supplier for advice.

Moving a WC Think hard before you settle on a room plan that involves moving a WC. Re-routeing a soil pipe is often impossible – maintaining the necessary fall on the pipe from WC to where it joins the main soil stack is very difficult. If moving the WC is your only option, you may need to consider fitting a macerator unit, that can pump the waste through narrower pipes.

ORDER OF WORK

• **Re-route pipework** to new positions.
• **Run cables** for wiring, but do not terminate at any of the fittings.
• **Paint the ceiling** before you install any new pieces of the bathroom suite to avoid dripping paint on the new fittings.
• **Fit the bath and shower tray.** It is a good idea to assemble as many of the fittings as you can before putting the bath in position, and it is essential to fit the waste trap and pipework as part of fitting the shower

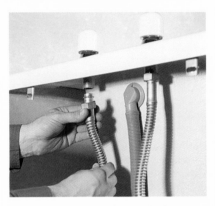

tray. Fix the taps to the bath, leaving their tails hanging loose, and attach the overflow assembly ready to be connected once the bath is in place.
• **Plumb in the mixer valve** for a mains-pressure shower.
• **Paint the walls.**
• **Tile the floor,** if appropriate.
• **Tile the walls** if the tiling is to run behind the WC.
• **Fit the WC and basin.**
• **Finish tiling the walls.**
• **Fit the shower and cubicle.**
• **Lay floor covering** if you are using vinyl or floor tiles.
• **Complete the wiring connections** for lights, shaver socket or any other electrical appliances.
• **Seal the joints** of all bathroom fittings with a bead of silicone.

Replacing a bidet or washbasin

The operations involved in replacing a washbasin or bidet are very similar. You may need to make slight adaptations to the existing plumbing to accommodate the new appliance.

Before you start You need to turn off the water supplies to the taps, and disconnect (or cut through) the supply and waste pipes. Then you can remove the fixings holding the basin (and its pedestal, if one is fitted) or bidet in place. Fit taps, wastes and overflows to the new basin or bidet before installing it.

Tools *Basin wrench; spanner; long-nose pliers; steel tape measure; spirit level; damp cloth; screwdriver; bucket. Possibly also hacksaw.*

Materials *Basin or bidet; taps or mixer with washers; appropriate trap (ask your plumbers' merchant); waste outlet with two flat plastic washers, plug and chain; silicone sealant; fixing screws for wall (and floor if required); rubber washers to fit between screws and appliance. Possibly also flexible pipe with tap connectors.*

HELPFUL TIP

If you want to renew the taps on an existing basin, it is often easier to cut through the supply and waste pipes and remove the basin from its supports. Even with a basin wrench, the back nuts can be extremely difficult to undo. With the basin upside down on the floor, it is easier to apply penetrating oil, and also to exert enough force without damaging the basin.

If removing the basin is not practical, the tap handles and headgear can be replaced with a tap conversion kit, sold in packs with fitting instructions.

2 If you severed the supply pipes, attach a corrugated copper pipe or braided hose connector to each new tap tail, ready for connection to the cut supply pipes later.

3 Attach the new waste outlet. Fit one sealing washer between the outlet and the appliance, then insert the outlet in its hole. Fit the second sealing washer from below and tighten the backnut. Use pliers to hold the outlet grid and stop the waste outlet from rotating as you do this. Ensure that the slots in the outlet tail line up with the outlet of the built-in overflow duct.

1 Fit the new taps or mixer. Place the sealing washer on the tap tail first, position the tap and screw on the backnut to secure the tap in place. Tighten it with a spanner. Check that single taps are correctly aligned.

4 Fit the trap to the tail of the waste outlet.

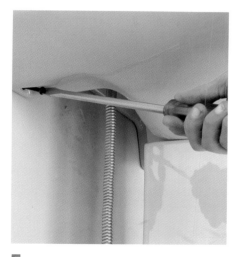

5 Set the new appliance in position and mark where new wall and floor fixings will be needed. Drill and plug the wall (and drill pilot holes in the floor too if necessary) and fix it in position.

6 Connect the taps or mixer to the supply pipes. If you disconnected the old tap connectors, there may be enough play in the pipes for you to reattach them directly to the new tap tails. If there is just a small gap, fit a tap tail adapter to each tap and attach the old tap connectors to the adapters. If you severed the supply pipes, link the flexible connectors you attached to the taps in step 2 to the supply pipes using compression fittings. Include a service valve on each pipe (see right) if none is fitted.

7 Connect the outlet at the base of the bottle trap to the waste pipe.

8 Restore the water supply and check all joints for leaks. If necessary, tighten them.

9 Run a bead of silicone sealant around the appliance where it meets the wall.

Connecting a washbasin If it is difficult to disconnect the water supplies to the taps on the old basin, cut through the pipes lower down and use flexible connectors to connect the new taps to the supply pipes. Fit a service valve between the connectors and the pipes at the same time so that you can isolate the taps easily for future maintenance.

An over-rim supply bidet is connected to the supply pipes in the same way as a basin. You will need adapters to connect the narrow tails of a monobloc mixer to 15mm diameter water supply pipes.

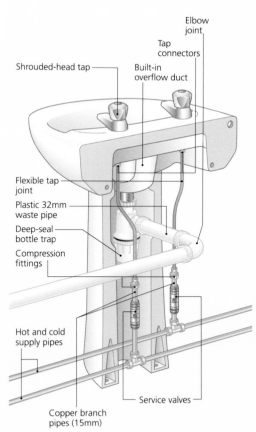

Shrouded-head tap

Elbow joint

Tap connectors

Built-in overflow duct

Flexible tap joint

Plastic 32mm waste pipe

Deep-seal bottle trap

Compression fittings

Hot and cold supply pipes

Service valves

Copper branch pipes (15mm)

Installing a countertop basin

Washbasins, particularly countertop basins on a vanity unit, are very often installed in a bedroom to ease the demand on a family bathroom.

Before you start Give the local authority Building Control Officer details of your proposed arrangements for the new waste pipe connections.

1 Choose a site for the basin as near as possible to the bathroom waste pipe and supply pipes – ideally against a wall adjoining the bathroom.

2 Work out how to route the waste water from the basin to an existing waste pipe or direct to an outside drain (see right). Trace the routes of existing hot and cold supply pipes and work out the shortest route possible for the new pipe.

3 Check that the basin position will allow sufficient space for a person to use it. Generally, allow at least 640mm bending room in front of the basin, and at least 300mm elbow room at either side.

4 Check that the installation of the basin will not interfere with any electric cables, gas pipes or other fittings, especially where you need to make a hole in a wall.

5 Fit the taps, waste outlet and trap to the new washbasin as described in Replacing a bidet or washbasin (page 96).

6 Cut off the water supply and use tee connectors to run hot and cold-water pipes to the basin site as 15mm branch pipes from the supply pipes to the bathroom. Do not tee into the pipes supplying a shower, unless it has a thermostatic mixer (page 93). If you find you have to tee into a 22mm distribution pipe, you will need an unequal tee with two 22mm ends and a 15mm branch.

7 Fit the waste pipe in position. You may have to make a hole through the wall. If you plan to connect the new waste pipe into an existing one, insert a swept tee joint and link the new pipe to it.

8 Fit the basin or basin unit to the wall and connect it to the supply pipes and waste pipe (see previous page).

Routeing the waste pipe

The waste pipe run should be no more than 1.75m long. It must slope enough for the water to run away – not less than 20mm for each 1m of run – but the depth of fall to the pipe outlet should be no greater than about 50mm for a pipe under 1m long, or about 25mm for a longer pipe. If you cannot avoid a pipe run longer than 1.75m, you should fit an anti-siphon bottle trap or a Hep$_2$O waste pipe valve (ask your plumbers' merchant for advice).

Alternatively Use a waste pipe of larger diameter – 38mm instead of 32mm. This pipe run should be no longer than 2.3m, and you will need a reducer fitting to connect 38mm pipe to the 32mm trap outlet. If you need a run longer than 2.3m, ask the advice of your local authority Building Control Officer.

HELPFUL TIPS

If you tee into an old distribution pipe, it is likely to be an imperial size of ³/₄in internal diameter. There is no way of recognising an imperial size, except by measuring the internal diameter of the pipe once you have cut into it.

On ³/₄in copper pipe, you can fit 22mm compression joints straight onto it provided that you substitute the olives for ³/₄in olives, available at a plumbers' merchant.

¾ in to 22mm adaptor

¾ in supply pipe

22mm tee joint

Flexible plastic push-fit joints are useful for fitting between the trap and waste pipe where alignment is difficult – for example, round a timber stud in a partition wall.

Linking to an outside drain

How the waste pipe is linked to a drain depends on the household drainage system. If you are unable to link into the waste pipe from the bathroom basin, fit a separate waste pipe through an outside wall to link with a household drain.

If the bedroom is on the ground floor, direct the waste pipe to an outside gully, if possible, such as the kitchen drain. The pipe must go below the grid.

Where the bedroom is on an upper floor, the method of connecting the waste pipe depends on whether you have a two-pipe or single-stack system (page 15).

With a two-pipe system, you may be able to direct the waste pipe into an existing hopper. Alternatively, you can connect the waste pipe to the waste downpipe (not the soil pipe) using a stack connector.

In a house with a single stack system, the waste pipe will have to be connected to the stack. For this you need the approval of the local authority Building Control Officer. There are regulations concerning the position of the connection in relation to WC inlets, and the length and slope of the pipe is particularly critical. The connection is made by fitting a new boss, which is a job best left to a plumber.

Bedroom basin installation

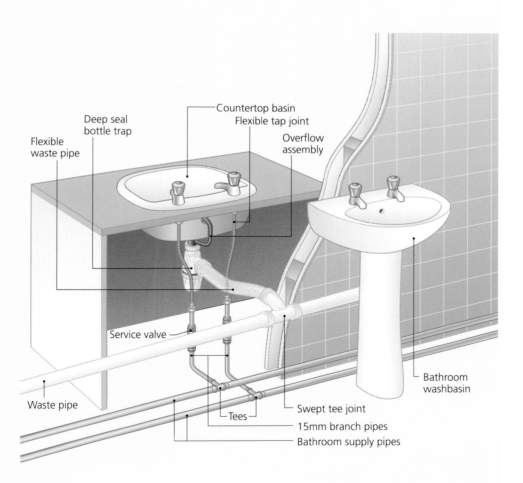

Deep seal bottle trap

Countertop basin
Flexible tap joint

Flexible waste pipe

Overflow assembly

Service valve

Waste pipe

Tees

Swept tee joint

15mm branch pipes

Bathroom supply pipes

Bathroom washbasin

Removing an old cast-iron bath

A cast-iron bath may weigh around 100kg, so you will need helpers to move it. A pressed-steel bath is lighter. It can usually be moved intact.

Before you start Unless you want to keep a cast-iron bath intact, it is easier to break it up after disconnecting it than to remove it whole. Be careful when you break it up, as the pieces are often jagged and very sharp.

Tools *Torch; adjustable spanner; safety goggles; ear defenders; club hammer; blanket; protective gloves. Possibly also padded pipe wrench; screwdriver; hacksaw.*

1 Cut off the water supply.

2 Remove any bath panelling. It is often secured with dome-head screws, which have caps that cover the screw slot.

3 With a torch, look into the space at the end of the bath to locate the supply pipes connected to the tap tails, and the overflow pipe. In older baths, the overflow pipe is rigid and leads straight out through the wall. In more modern types the overflow is flexible and connected to the waste trap.

4 Check the position of the hot supply pipe: it is normally on the left as you face the taps. Use an adjustable spanner to unscrew the tap connectors from the supply pipes and pull the pipes to one side. If unscrewing is difficult, saw through the pipes near the ends of the tap tails.

5 Saw through a rigid overflow pipe flush with the wall.

6 Disconnect the waste trap from the waste outlet. For an old-style U-bend, use an adjustable spanner. A plastic trap can normally be unscrewed by hand, but use a padded pipe wrench if it proves difficult. Pull the trap to one side. Disconnect a flexible overflow pipe from the overflow outlet.

7 If the bath has adjustable legs – normally brackets with adjustable screws and locking nuts – lower it to lessen the risk of damaging wall tiles when you pull it out. But if the adjusters on the far side are

difficult to reach, lowering may not be worth the effort.

8 Pull the bath into the middle of the room ready for removal or break-up.

9 To break up the bath, drape a blanket over it to stop fragments flying out, and hit the sides with a club hammer to crack the material into pieces.

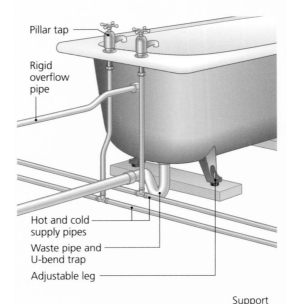

Pillar tap

Rigid overflow pipe

Hot and cold supply pipes

Waste pipe and U-bend trap

Adjustable leg

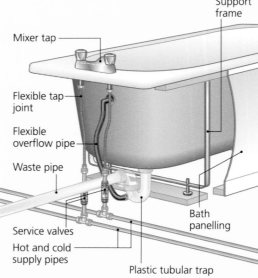

Support frame

Mixer tap

Flexible tap joint

Flexible overflow pipe

Waste pipe

Service valves

Hot and cold supply pipes

Plastic tubular trap

Bath panelling

Connections to an old and new bath
As when replacing a washbasin or bidet (page 96), add a service valve on each of the supply pipes before connecting them to the new taps. This allows them to be isolated easily for future maintenance.

Installing a bath

Assemble as many fittings as possible onto the new bath before you remove the old one. Fitting is easier before the bath is in position and the water will not be cut off for as long.

Use flexible connectors and a flexible waste joint. If you want to reposition the bath, you will have to work out how to re-route the waste and supply pipes.

Tools *Two adjustable spanners; spirit level; damp cloth. Possibly also long nosed pliers; small spanner; hacksaw; screwdriver.*

Materials *Bath; two 25mm thick boards to support its feet; two new taps or a mixer tap (with washers); two 22mm flexible pipe connectors; 40mm waste outlet with plug and two flat plastic washers; bath trap with flexible overflow assembly; silicone sealant; PTFE tape.*

1 Fit the supporting frame following the maker's instructions. It is usually done with the bath placed upside down. Fit the taps or mixer and the tap joints in the same way as for a washbasin. Some deck mixers come with a plastic gasket to fit between the deck and the bath. On a plastic bath, fit a reinforcing plate under the taps to prevent strain on the bath deck.

2 Fit the waste outlet. This may be a tailed grid fitted in the same way as for a sink. Or it may be a flanged grid only, fitted over the outlet hole (with washers on each side of the bath) and fixed with a screw to a tail at one end of the flexible overflow pipe.

3 Fit the top end of the overflow pipe into the back of the overflow hole and screw the overflow outlet, backed by a washer, in position.

4 Slot the banjo overflow, if supplied, onto the threaded waste outlet and fit the bottom washer and back nut. Attach the trap, then fit the bath into position with a flat board under each pair of feet in order to spread the load.

5 Place a spirit level on each of the four sides of the bath to check that it is horizontal. If necessary, adjust the legs until the bath is perfectly level. Then tighten the locking nuts on the adjustable legs.

6 Fit the flexible connector on the farthest tap to its supply pipe, making a compression joint. If the supply pipe is too high, cut it back to a convenient length, leaving it too long rather than too short, as the connector can be bent slightly to fit.

7 Connect the second tap tail in the same way as the first. Then connect the trap outlet to the waste pipe (normally a push-fit joint). Restore the water supply and check the joints for leaks. Tighten if necessary, but not too much.

8 Fix the bath panels according to the maker's instructions. They may screw or clip to a wooden frame, or be fixed to a batten screwed to the floor. Fill the bath with water before sealing the joints between the bath sides and walls with silicone sealant. This ensures that the bath will not settle in use and pull the sealant away.

Replacing a WC

At one time WC pans were always cemented to a solid floor. Now they are usually screwed down to a wooden or a solid floor. Modern WCs with close-coupled cisterns are quite straightforward to install – but first you need to remove the old pan.

Before you start An old WC with a down-pointing outlet cemented to a floor-exit soil pipe is difficult to remove; Newer types are far easier to take out. Start by uncoupling and removing the cistern (page 35).

Tools *Adjustable spanner; screwdriver; spirit level. Power drill with wood and masonry bits; safety goggles; club hammer; cold chisel; rags; old chisel; thin pencil; trimming knife; junior hacksaw.*

Materials *Close-coupled WC suite; suitable pan joint (see right); silicone grease. Wall plugs and screws; push-fit tap joint; packing, such as wood slivers or silicone sealant (to level the pan); perhaps nylon pan fixings; toilet seat.*

Removing a pan with a horizontal outlet

1 Turn off the water supply and protect floor with a thick layer of old dustsheets or newspaper. Have an empty bucket to hand.

2 Disconnect the flush pipe by peeling back the cone connector. Alternatively, chip away a rag-and-putty joint with an old chisel. Protect your eyes.

3 Undo any screws used to secure the pan to the floor.

4 Pull the pan towards you slowly, moving it from side to side, to free it from the soil-pipe inlet. It should come away easily. Tip any residual water into the bucket. If it does not come away easily, break the pan outlet in the same way as for a down-pointing outlet (right).

5 If the outlet joint was cemented with putty or mastic filler, clean it off the metal soil pipe inlet using an old chisel. Tape a carrier bag over the exposed soil pipe to keep out the worst of the drain odour.

Removing a pan with a down-pointing outlet

1 Disconnect the flush pipe in the same way as for a horizontal-outlet pan, then undo the floor screws, or break cement with a hammer and cold chisel.

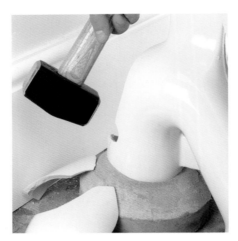

2 To free the pan outlet, put on safety goggles and use a club hammer to break the outlet pipe just above its joint with the drain socket in the floor. Then pull the pan forward, away from the jagged remains protruding from the soil pipe socket.

3 Stuff rags into the socket to stop debris falling in and to contain the smell from the soil pipe. Chip away the rest of the pan outlet with a hammer and cold chisel. If you work with the chisel blade pointing inwards, and break the china right down to the socket at one point, the rest of the china should come out easily.

4 Taking care not to break the collar, chip away any mortar from round the collar of the socket with a hammer and cold chisel.

5 Clear away any mortar left where the pan was cemented to the floor, leaving a flat base for the new WC pan.

Putting together a close-coupled WC

1 Assemble the flush mechanism following the manufacturer's instructions. Be sure to include any required rubber sealing rings.

2 Fit the flush mechanism into the cistern, and insert the cold water inlet valve assembly. Make sure that its rubber washer is securely in place inside the cistern; then fix in place using the supplied nut. Tighten by hand, then give an extra half turn using an adjustable spanner; do not overtighten.

3 Insert the long fixing bolts through the holes in the bottom of the cistern. Thread bolts through the fat rubber washers and large metal washers supplied.

4 Fit the large rubber gasket (sometimes known as a doughnut) into the flush entrance of the pan or onto the base of the cistern – according to WC manufacturer's instructions.

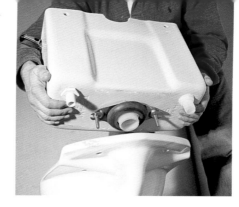

5 Lift the cistern onto the pan. The connecting bolts will fit through the holes at the back of the pan and the flush mechanism fits through the rubber gasket into the flush entrance of the pan.

6 Thread washers onto the connecting bolts beneath the back of the pan followed by the wing nuts. Hand tighten but, do not overtighten, or you risk cracking the china.

7 Carefully move the whole assembly into position.

TYPES OF WC PAN JOINTS

Plastic push-fit joints are now universally used and come in a variety of shapes to allow connection of virtually any pan to any soil pipe. Most joints are either straight or 90° (for horizontal or vertical soil pipes), but offset joints, extension joints and even fully flexible joints are also available.

Straight push-fit pan joint For a straight link between the pan outlet and the inlet branch to the soil pipe. The cupped end fits over the pan outlet, and the narrow (spigot) end inside the soil-pipe inlet. Different diameters and lengths are made. Before buying, check the outside diameter of the pan outlet, the inside diameter of the soil-pipe inlet, and the distance to be bridged. Joints have watertight seals at each end. Offset types can be used where the alignment is not exact.

Angled push-fit pan joint
A 90° joint for converting a horizontal (P-trap) pan outlet to a down-pointing (S-trap) outlet for a floor-exit pipe. It can also be used to link a horizontal outlet to a wall-exit pipe situated at right angles to the pan.

Rubber cone joint
For linking the flush pipe from the WC cistern to the flush horn of the pan.

Flush pipe Angled plastic pipe linking a separate cistern to the WC pan. Pipes for high-level suites are normally 32mm in diameter, and pipes for low-level suites have 38mm diameters.

Installing a close-coupled WC

1 Choose the right type of adapter to match the existing soil pipe. You will need a straight connector if the pipe passes through the wall immediately behind the pan, and a right-angled one otherwise.

2 You can fix the pan into position with screws – fitted with special inserts to protect the china – or with nylon pan fixings. With the pan in position, draw a line round its base and mark the positions of the fixing holes with a thin pencil, pen or bradawl. If the cistern has fixing holes at the back, mark these positions on the wall, too. Then move the assembly aside.

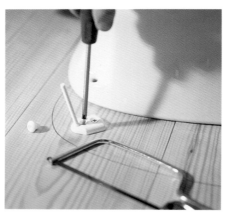

3 Drill and fix the pan fixings so that the plastic thread lines up with the marks on the floor; or drill screw holes into the floor. On a concrete or quarry tiled floor, use a masonry bit and insert wall plugs for the screws. Drill and plug holes in the wall for the cistern.

4 Remove plastic bags or rags from the soil pipe inlet and fit the appropriate flexible connector.

5 Carefully lift the assembly into position using the marked outline to guide you. Position it so that you can slide the pan outlet into the flexible connector. Apply a little silicone grease to help ease it in. If you have used nylon pan fixings, the threads will now protrude through the holes in the base of the pan. Fix the cistern to the wall.

6 Trim the threads to length and screw on the plastic nuts to hold the pan firmly in position. Or push protective plastic inserts through the base of the pan and fix it to the floor with screws. In either case, do not tighten fully, yet.

7 Using a spirit level placed across the top of the pan, check that it is level from side to side and from front to back. Correct the level by loosening the plastic nuts or screws and packing under the pedestal with slivers of wood, or use a bead of silicone sealant. Then screw it down firmly.

8 Connect the cold water supply to the cistern using a plastic push-fit tap joint. These incorporate rubber O-rings for sealing and are simply pushed into place. They can be used to join copper and plastic pipes.

(See page 37 for fitting a toilet seat.)

Installing a shower

Most types of shower can be fitted either over a bath or in a cubicle. The fixings and pipe routes vary according to the shower type, the bathroom layout and the shower location, but the method of installation is basically the same.

Before you start Decide on the type of shower you want (pages 92–93). Remember that the shower head must either be fitted so as to prevent it coming into contact with water in the bath or shower tray, or it must have a check valve (non-return valve) where the hose is attached to the shower control.

1 Mark the required positions of the spray head and shower control.

2 Plan the pipework to the shower control and how the waste water will be routed to the drainage system.

3 Fit the shower control. Most units are available as either surface-mounted or recessed fittings, and come with fixings and instructions.
   When fitting a recessed mixer, if possible mount it on a removable panel flush with the wall so that you have easy access to the controls.

4 Cut off the water supply and fit the water supply pipes. You can recess the pipes into the wall and then replaster or tile over them. However, they must be protected with a waterproof covering and have accessible service valves fitted.

5 Fit the shower head and spray. For a separate cubicle, fit the base tray and waste fittings.

6 Connect the supply pipes to the shower control. An adapter with a female screw thread (copper to iron) may be needed.

7 Restore the water supply and check the piping for leaks. Tighten any joints as necessary.

8 Fit screening panels and seal the joints between the wall and screening and the tray.

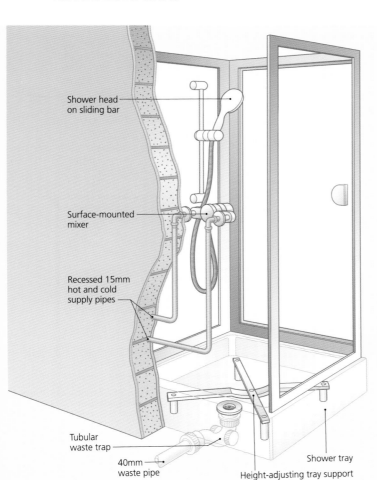

Shower head on sliding bar

Surface-mounted mixer

Recessed 15mm hot and cold supply pipes

Tubular waste trap

40mm waste pipe

Shower tray

Height-adjusting tray support

A typical cubicle installation
Screens are usually about 1.8m high. Panel widths can usually be adjusted by 25–50mm to allow for walls that are out of true. Doors may be hinged, folded (with panels shaped to keep water in), sliding with corner entry, or pivoted to give a wide entry without taking a lot of opening space. Some shower trays have an adjustable support by which the height can be altered so that the waste pipe and trap can be positioned either above or below the floorboards.

🔌 Wiring in new appliances

For safety, any electrical appliances installed in a bathroom must be run from a fused connection unit outside the room. Follow these instructions for preparing the wiring for an electrically heated towel rail, oil-filled radiator or a shaver socket.

For a towel rail or radiator, the cable runs from the back of the flex-outlet plate to a switched fused connection unit (FCU) outside the bathroom. A shaver socket is connected directly to the FCU. The FCU is fitted on a spur led from a socket outlet on the ring main circuit, as shown (right).

Tools *Suitable tools for preparing the route; sharp knife; pliers; insulated screwdrivers; wire cutters and strippers.*

Materials *Two standard single mounting boxes; 2.5mm² two-core-and-earth cable; cable clips; green-and-yellow sleeving for the earth cores; FCU; 13amp cartridge fuse; flex outlet plate; towel rail or radiator fixed on the wall.*

Preparation

1 Check that all the metallic parts in the room – radiator pipes, copper pipework to taps or bath, an enamelled cast iron or steel bath – are cross-bonded to earth with special screw-on earth clamps. If in doubt, have your earthing system checked by a qualified electrician.

2 Turn off the power at the consumer unit and remove the fuse or switch off the MCB protecting the circuit you want to work on.

3 Find a suitable supply socket outlet from which to run the spur. You must not use one that is already supplying a spur or is itself supplied as a spur. Remove the faceplate and undo the terminal screws to release the conductors.

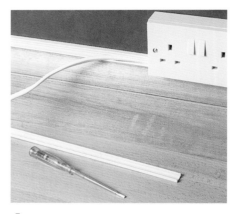

4 Prepare the route. This may involve lifting floorboards, cutting a channel into plaster or fixing surface-mounted trunking (above). Lead the spur cable from the supply socket outlet to the wall outside the bathroom where the FCU will be sited, and from there to the bathroom wall where the flex outlet plate is to be fixed.

5 Prepare recesses for the mounting boxes for the FCU and the flex outlet plate. Fix two lengths of cable in place, one from the supply socket to the FCU, the other from the FCU to the flex outlet plate.

EARTH SAFETY

Proper earthing of any metal parts you can touch on electrical equipment and appliances provides vital protection from the risk of electric shock. Metal parts include the screws holding on the faceplate of a socket or switch, pipework, radiators, some baths, and heated towel rails. Where copper pipes are joined with plastic connectors (which break the earth circuit), earth cable must be attached so as to bridge the join in order to maintain the circuit. All metal items in a bathroom must be connected together using 4mm² earth cable and bonded to the house earth system.

Wiring outside the bathroom

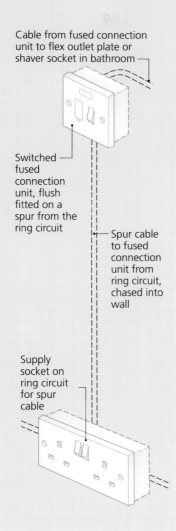

Cable from fused connection unit to flex outlet plate or shaver socket in bathroom

Switched fused connection unit, flush fitted on a spur from the ring circuit

Spur cable to fused connection unit from ring circuit, chased into wall

Supply socket on ring circuit for spur cable

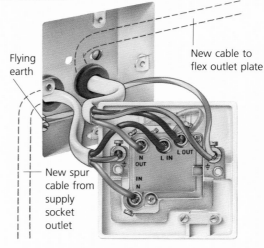

Flying earth

New cable to flex outlet plate

New spur cable from supply socket outlet

N OUT   L IN   L OUT

IN N

Connecting at the FCU

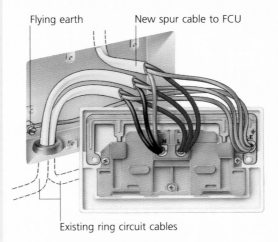

Flying earth

New spur cable to FCU

Existing ring circuit cables

Connecting at the supply socket

6 Feed the ends of the cables into the mounting boxes after fitting grommets in the knock-out holes. Screw the boxes into place. Feed the end of the appliance flex through to the back of the flex outlet plate. Prepare the new cable and the flex cores for connection.

7 Repair the plaster and wait for it to dry. Replace any floorboards.

Connecting at the socket outlet

1 Match the cores of the three cables – red from the ring circuit with brown from the new cables, black from the ring circuit with blue from the new cables and green-and-yellow with green-and-yellow.

2 Screw the sets of conductors into the correct terminals – red and brown at L, black and blue at N and green-and-yellow at E or ⏚.

3 Add a flying earth link between the earth terminals on the faceplate and in the mounting box. See illustration above.

4 Press the socket onto the mounting box without disturbing the conductors and screw it in place.

Connecting at the FCU

1 Connect the cable from the supply socket to the FCU. The brown (live) core goes to the terminal marked L and Mains (or Supply, Feed or In). The blue (neutral) core goes to N and Mains (or Supply, Feed or In). The green-and-yellow earth core goes to the nearer of the two terminals marked E or ⏚. If the FCU has only one earth terminal, do not connect it yet.

2 Connect the cable leading from the FCU to the flex outlet plate. The brown (live) core goes to the terminal marked L and Load (or Out), the blue core to N and Load (or Out), and the green-and-yellow-sleeved earth core to the second terminal marked E or ⏚. If there is only one earth terminal, connect both earth cores to it.

3 Add a flying earth link between the earth terminals on the faceplate and in the mounting box.

Wiring inside the bathroom

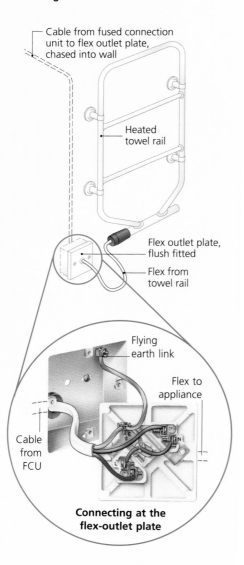

Cable from fused connection unit to flex outlet plate, chased into wall

Heated towel rail

Flex outlet plate, flush fitted

Flex from towel rail

Flying earth link

Flex to appliance

Cable from FCU

Connecting at the flex-outlet plate

4 Fit the 13amp fuse in the fuseholder in the FCU faceplate and screw the faceplate to the mounting box. Do not overtighten the screws or the plastic may crack.

5 Then connect the cable that runs from the FCU to the flex outlet plate or shaver socket in the bathroom.

SUPPLEMENTARY ELECTRICAL HEATING

This wiring is also used for modern ladder radiators (below), which are designed to heat up with the central heating system in winter, but can be overridden with an electric element in summer or when the central heating is switched off.

✋ Connecting a heated towel rail

The flex for an electrical appliance in a bathroom must be wired into a flex outlet plate that does not have a switch.

1 Run a cable from a fused connection unit (FCU) outside the bathroom to the position of the flex outlet plate. Fit a recessed mounting box into the wall and feed the cable into it then connect the new cable at the FCU and the flex outlet plate.

2 Connect the flex cores to one set of terminals – brown to L, blue to N, and green-and-yellow to E or ⏚.

3 Connect the cable cores in the same way to the other set of terminals.

4 Add a flying earth link between the earth terminals on the faceplate and in the mounting box. Screw the faceplate to the mounting box.

✋ Fitting a shaver point

The only electric socket outlet permitted in a bathroom is a shaver point. You can connect it to the main power supply via an FCU outside the bathroom.

• There are purpose-made mounting boxes for shaver supply units. Surface-mounted boxes are available but it is safer to fit a flush-mounted metal box into the wall.
• You can install the unit on a spur led from a suitable existing socket outlet on a ring main circuit.
• The preparation and general principles of installing a shaver supply unit on a spur

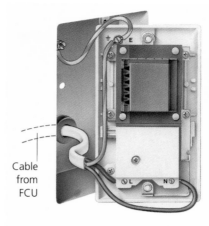

Cable from FCU

Connecting at the shaver point

from a ring-main circuit are the same as those described for connecting heated towel rails or radiators at the supply socket or FCU. In the bathroom, connect the cable run from the FCU to the shaver socket (above).

Installing a shaver point on a lighting spur

It is also common to install a shaver socket on a spur led from a junction box inserted in the lighting circuit above the bathroom.

1 Lead the spur cable from the lighting circuit to the shaver supply unit position, using 1mm² twin-core-and-earth cable. (Note that when fitting the junction box – unless your house has been rewired since 2006 or is newly built – the existing lighting circuit will have a red (live) core and a black (neutral) core. Connect the new brown core to red, blue to black and earth to earth.)

2 Fit the mounting box for the shaver supply unit at about shoulder height on the wall. Feed in the cable through a grommet.

3 Prepare the end of the cable and connect the cores into the terminals on the shaver supply unit faceplate – brown to L, blue to N, and green-and-yellow to E or ⏚.

4 Fold the cable neatly into the mounting box and screw on the faceplate. Restore the power supply to the lighting circuit.

Finishing touches

Preparing the surface

The glaze on tiles will highlight even tiny undulations in a wall so the surface must be as flat as possible.

Plaster
Sound, bare plaster is an ideal surface for tiling. The tile adhesive will fill minor cracks and holes; patch larger defects with a skim of ready-mixed repair plaster. Hack off any hollow areas and replaster them. Seal the surface with plaster primer. Scrape any loose paint from painted plaster. Key gloss-painted walls with coarse wet-and-dry abrasive paper.

Plasterboard
You can tile over painted plasterboard; seal bare plasterboard with two coats of emulsion paint. Use water-resistant boards such as Aquapanel instead of ordinary plasterboard for shower cubicle walls.

Papered walls
Strip all wallcoverings before tiling, and seal bare surfaces as described above.

Worktops
Before tiling a laminated worktop, score it with a metal abrasive disc fitted to a power drill. Coarse abrasive paper or a file will also do the job but will take longer.

Old ceramic tiles
You can tile over old tiles so long as they are securely bonded to the surface behind. Remove any loose tiles and fill the recess with repair plaster. Wash the surface with sugar soap to remove grease and soap deposits.

Man-made boards
Seal board surfaces with wood primer or diluted PVA building adhesive. Use moisture-resistant boards for bath panels and similar uses in damp areas.

GROUT AND SEALANT
Tile adhesive and grout come in several forms. The most widely used is an all-in-one ready-mixed product that sticks the tiles and fills the joints, and is water and mould-resistant. It is an ideal choice for most tiling jobs. One 10-litre tub will cover an area of 10–12m².

Separate grouts and adhesives You can also buy adhesive and grout as separate products, in ready-mixed or powder form, which you mix with water. Do this only if you want to use coloured grout, or if you are tiling a kitchen worktop where a special epoxy grout is recommended for hygiene reasons. Powder products are cheaper than ready-mixed options, so may be worth considering for large tiling projects.

Sealing joints Use flexible mastic, not grout, to seal the joints between tiles and bathroom fittings or kitchen worktops (a special flexible beaded trim is also available for this purpose). Use mastic also to fill internal corners and the joins between tiles and skirting boards or door architraves.

Tile spacers X-shaped plastic spacers are essential for spacing tiles evenly. They come in sizes from 2 to 5mm thick. Use 2mm spacers with 100mm square tiles, and larger sizes with bigger tiles.

Planning the tile layout

Whether you are tiling a simple splashback or an entire wall, deciding where to start is always the first step. Because an area of tiling is made up of regular units, it always looks best if the tile pattern is centred on the wall – or in the case of a splashback, on the washbasin, sink or bath that it is complementing.

Tiling around a bath

A bath is usually sited either in a corner or in an alcove. If the bath fits exactly in an alcove, the tiling should finish in line with the front edge of the bath at the head and foot; if it is in a corner, the tiling should finish flush with the front edge and the end of the bath.

1 Start each row with a whole tile at the outer edge of the bath or alcove. Centre the tiling on the back wall.

2 Once all the whole tiles are in place, finish the rows with cut tiles in each internal corner.

Tiling a splashback

A simple splashback for a washbasin or sink usually consists of two or three rows of tiles on the wall above it. Because the tiled area is self-contained, you can complete the job using only whole tiles. There are two choices for centring the tile layout (below). If the basin is in an alcove, centre the tiles in the alcove, positioning cut tiles of equal width at either edge.

1 Mark the centre of the basin or sink on the wall above and draw a vertical line there. Place a whole tile at either side of the line, then add more whole tiles in a row until the tiling reaches (or extends just beyond) the edge of the basin or sink (below). Add a second or third row of tiles to complete the splashback.

2 If this layout means that tiles finish just short of the edges of the basin or sink or extend too far on either side, place the first

tile astride the centre line instead (see diagram). This has the effect of moving the tile row along by half the width of a tile, and may create a better-looking layout. Add extra rows of tiles to reach the required height.

Half-tiling a wall

You can set out and centre tiles for a splashback by eye, standing tiles in a row along the back edge of the fixture to work out the best layout. On a wall, a simple aid called a tiling gauge makes the setting out much easier.

Tiling a wall to a height of about 1.2m is a popular project in a bathroom or separate WC. If the wall is unobstructed, the centring rule is simple to apply. Each row should have cut tiles of equal width at each end (except in the unlikely event that a row of whole tiles exactly fills the available space). Each column will have a whole tile at the top and a cut tile at the bottom.

You may be tempted to save work and start each column with a whole tile at floor or skirting board level, but there is a good reason why you should not do this. The floor or skirting board may not be truly level, and the effect of using it as a base-line will gradually force the tile rows and columns off square. You might get away with this on a single tiled wall, but if you are tiling all round the room the cumulative effect can be disastrous.

Positioning tiles for a splashback

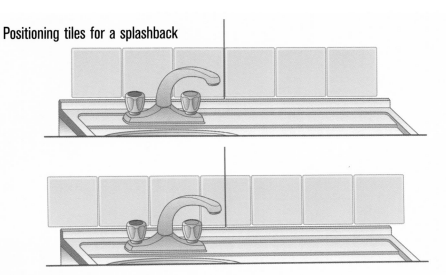

Using guide battens

The secret of success is to use a horizontal timber guide batten fixed to the wall beneath the bottom edge of the lowest row of whole tiles. Position it so that the gap to be filled between this row and the floor or skirting board is about three-quarters of a tile width.

You have to place all the whole tiles on the wall before you can fit any cut tiles at the ends of the rows. It is therefore a good idea to add a vertical guide batten at one side of the area, to ensure that the columns of tiles are all precisely vertical. Once all the whole tiles have been placed, both the vertical and horizontal battens are removed so the cut tiles can be measured, cut and fixed in place.

Using a tiling gauge

1 Measure the width of the wall to be tiled and mark the centre point. Hold the tile gauge horizontally, with one end less than a tile width from a corner, and align a joint mark with the centre line. If the gap at the end of the gauge is between one-third and two-thirds of a tile wide, you have a satisfactory tile layout. Mark the wall in line with the end of the gauge. This indicates where the vertical guide batten will be fixed.

2 If the gap is very narrow, or is almost a whole tile wide, it will be difficult to cut tiles to fit. You will get a better layout by moving the gauge along by half a tile width. Do this, then mark the wall in line with the end of the gauge to indicate where to fix the vertical guide batten.

3 Hold the gauge vertically to assess where the top of the tiled area will finish. Move it up so the bottom of the gauge is about three-quarters of a tile width above the floor or skirting board. Mark the wall at a joint mark to indicate the top of the tiled area. Make another mark level with the bottom of the gauge to indicate the level of the horizontal guide batten.

Fixing the battens

You now have pencil marks on the wall indicating the level of the lowest row of whole tiles, and also the edge of the column of whole tiles nearest the room corner.

1 Fix the horizontal guide batten first, using a spirit level to get it truly horizontal. If you are tiling more than one wall, fix guide battens to each wall, and check that they are precisely aligned with each other.

2 Use a spirit level to mark a true vertical line down to the horizontal guide batten from the end mark you made on the wall with your tiling gauge.

3 Fix a vertical guide batten at this point, long enough to reach up to the top of the area to be tiled. Secure the battens with

MAKING A TILING GAUGE

To make it, you need a piece of 50 x 25mm planed softwood about 2m long. Choose a piece that is straight and not warped in either direction. Place it on the floor and lay a row of tiles alongside it, with tile spacers between the tiles to create uniform gaps of the correct width. Mark a pencil line on the batten to coincide with each joint. Cut the gauge to length at the last pencil mark. You can then hold the gauge against the wall to see how whole tiles will fit in the space available. It is also invaluable for centring tiles on walls with obstacles such as windows, doors and bathroom or kitchen equipment (see page 117).

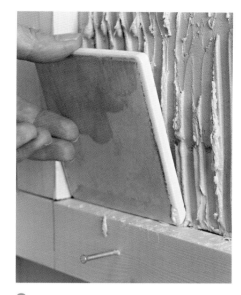

masonry nails on solid walls, and with wire nails on timber-framed partitions. Leave the nail heads projecting by about 10mm so they can be pulled out easily when it is time to remove the battens.

Tiling a wall

With the setting-out complete and the guide battens fixed, you can start to place the whole tiles on the wall. Put down a dust sheet to catch stray blobs of adhesive, unpack your tiles and spacers and place them nearby.

Tools *Notched spreader; stripping knife; damp cloth.*

Materials *Tiles; tile adhesive; spacers.*

1 Scoop some adhesive from the tub with your spreader and spread it on the wall in a band a little more than one tile wide. The notches form ridges in the adhesive which will be compressed to an even thickness as you place the tiles.

2 Place the first tile in the angle between the guide battens. Rest its lower edge on the horizontal batten, then press it into the adhesive. Check that its edge is against the vertical batten.

3 Place more tiles one by one along the row, fitting a spacer between them, until you reach the room corner. Press the spacers at the top corners into the adhesive so they will be covered when you fill the joints with grout (page 120). At the bottom corners, push one leg of each spacer into the gap between the tiles; these will be pulled out when the batten is removed.

4 Hold the edge of your tiling gauge across the faces of the tiles to check that they are flush with each other. Press in any that are proud of their neighbours.

5 Apply another band of adhesive and place the second row of tiles. Align the bottom edge of each one between the spacers in the row below before pressing it into place. Then fit spacers between the top corners as before.

6 When you have placed the topmost row of tiles, scrape off any excess adhesive from the wall with a stripping knife and wipe off the remaining traces with a damp cloth.

7 Allow the adhesive to set for 24 hours. Then prise out the nails that are holding the guide battens in place, taking care not to dislodge the tiles. Measure and cut individual tiles, one at a time, to fit the width of the remaining gaps (see below) and butter some adhesive onto the back with your spreader.

8 Fit spacers into the gaps between the rows of whole tiles. Then fit the cut pieces, one at a time, into the gap between the spacers. Press the cut tile into place so its face is flush with its neighbour. Repeat the process, measuring, cutting and fitting the remaining tiles at both ends of each row. Then cut tiles to fill the gap between the bottom row of whole tiles and the skirting board or floor.

Cutting tiles to fit

Tiling a splashback is easy – you probably won't even have to cut a tile. But if you are tiling a whole wall, you will encounter various obstacles.

Tools *Chinagraph pencil; steel rule; platform tile cutter; tile saw; tile nibbler; pencil; G-cramp.*

Materials *Tiles; adhesive.*

Taking a sliver off a tile

1 Platform tile cutters will not make fine cuts less than 15mm wide. Use a hand-held tile scorer and steel straightedge. Score the tile much more deeply than for an ordinary cut – you need to cut right through the glaze in order to get a clean break.

2 Nibble away at the sliver of tile that is being removed, using a tile nibbler. Smooth any sharp edges with a tile file.

Finishing a row

1 When you reach the end of a row, place the final tile over the previous tile and butt it up to the corner. Allow for the width of a grout joint and mark the cutting line.

2 Use a platform tile cutter to make a neat straight cut. Score the tile with the cutting wheel then use the lever to snap the tile along the line. Position the tile on the wall with the cut edge into the corner.

3 Measure the final tile in each row separately. Few walls are perfectly square, so your measurements are unlikely to be the same all the way up.

Cutting a curved line

1 Cut a piece of paper to the size of a tile to make a template to fit around the curved object.

2 Make a series of cuts in the edge that will butt up to the obstacle. Press the tongues against the obstacle so that the creases define its outline.

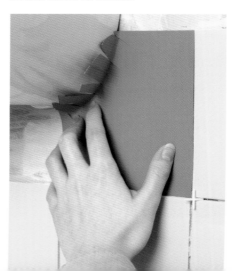

3 Use the paper as a guide to transfer the curved line with a chinagraph pencil onto the glazed tile surface.

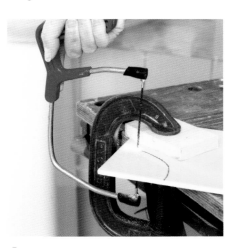

4 Clamp the tile face-up to a workbench, protecting the glaze with a board offcut sandwiched between tile and cramp. Cut along the marked line with a tile saw. Work slowly and with as little pressure as possible to avoid chipping the glaze. File away any excess if necessary to get a perfect fit.

POWER CUTS FOR TILES

If you have a craft drill, such as a Dremel, you can use its tile-cutting attachment to make holes in tiles. Mark the cutting line as described overleaf, but don't split the tile in two until after you have made the hole. Cut out the circle you have marked then split the tile and fit it.

POSITIONING TILES AROUND A WINDOW

Tiles look best if they are centred around a window opening. Use a tiling gauge (page 114) to span the window and adjust its position until there is an equal width of tile on either side of the opening. Mark the wall to indicate the outer edge of the tiles that will need to be cut. Drop a plumb line through the first of the lines to transfer the mark to the horizontal batten at the bottom of the wall. Work from this mark towards the corner of the room, measuring full tile widths and grout joints to determine the position of the last whole tile in each row. Fix the vertical batten to the wall at this point.

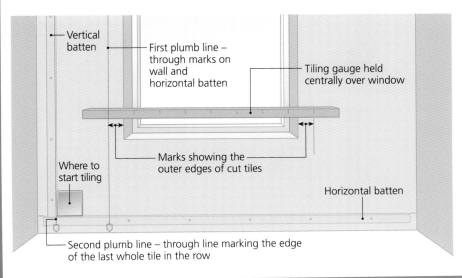

Vertical batten

First plumb line – through marks on wall and horizontal batten

Tiling gauge held centrally over window

Marks showing the outer edges of cut tiles

Where to start tiling

Horizontal batten

Second plumb line – through line marking the edge of the last whole tile in the row

Making holes

1 When you tile around plumbing – in a shower, for example – you may need to make holes in the tiles to allow pipes to run through. Offer up the tile from the side and from below, and mark each edge in line with the centre of the pipe. Draw straight lines to extend the marks: where they intersect is the pipe centre. Trace round an offcut of pipe – or a coin or other round object of about the same diameter – to mark a cutting line at this point.

2 Cut the tile in two along one of the lines drawn through the centre of the marked pipe hole. Score the outline of each resulting semi-circle with a pencil-type tile cutter. Use a tile nibbler to cut the hole.

3 Fit the two cut pieces together around the pipe. Grout around the pipe or use a silicone sealant for a water-tight finish.

Tiling around corners

Internal corners

Place all the whole tiles on both walls, then remove the guide battens so that you can cut and fit the tiles in the corner.

1 Measure and cut a tile to fit the width of the gap to be filled (page 116). Butter the back of the cut tile with adhesive and press it into place with the cut edge facing into the corner.

2 When the adhesive has dried, seal the angle between the two walls with a flexible waterproof mastic. This will allow for a little wall movement over time. Use masking tape to mask the joint, apply the mastic, smooth it and peel off the tape once a skin has formed.

External corners

External corners should, ideally, start with whole tiles on each wall, though this is unlikely to be possible at a window rebate. Joins can be made by butting the tiles, using plastic corner trim or sticking on a strip of timber beading.

2 Start tiling the second wall, easing each tile into the corner trim as you place it. Don't push it too hard – you don't want to dislodge the trim. When you have laid all the corner tiles, make sure the trim lines up with the tile faces on both walls.

Butt joint A simple overlapping butt joint works well if the corner is true and the tiles have glazed edges. Tile the less visible wall first, placing whole tiles flush with the corner. Then tile the other wall, overlapping these tiles to conceal the edges of those on the first wall.

Plastic corner trim Coloured plastic or chrome corner trims will protect tiles on external corners from damage and give the edge a neat finish. You can use the trim along the edges of tiled door and window recesses as well.

A window recess

1 Tile the wall as far as the window, cutting tiles to fit. If you have to cut a tile to an L shape, cut a line from the edge to the centre of the tile using a tile saw then score a line at right angles to the cut and snap off the unwanted piece. Use lengths of plastic edging strip designed for external corners to give the edges a neat finish.

2 Lay the tiles at the bottom of the recess first. Put any cut tiles nearest the window, with cut edges against the frame.

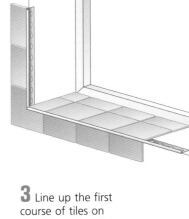

1 Push the perforated base of the trim into the tile adhesive on one corner so that the outer edge of the rounded trim lines up perfectly with the faces of the tiles on the adjacent wall.

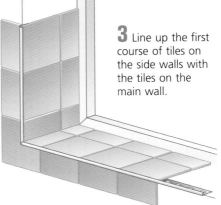

3 Line up the first course of tiles on the side walls with the tiles on the main wall.

Grouting between tiles

When the tiles have been in place for at least 12 hours, fill the gaps between them with grout. This gives an attractive finished appearance and prevents dirt from collecting in the cracks.

Tools *Pieces of sponge or a squeegee; larger sponge; thin dowel or something similar for finishing; soft dry cloth.*

Materials *Grout (waterproof for kitchens or bathrooms).*

1 If the grout is not ready-mixed, prepare as recommended. With waterproof epoxy-based grout, mix only a little at a time – it sets hard quickly.

2 Press the grout firmly into the gaps between the tiles. Professionals use a rubber-edged squeegee, but if you have never grouted before you may find it easier to get the grout well into the cracks with a small piece of sponge.

HELPFUL TIP

Revive discoloured grout by painting it with a proprietary liquid grout whitener, applied with an artist's brush. Be aware, though, that this is a slow and tedious job.

3 Wipe away any grout that gets onto the surface of the tiles with a clean, damp sponge while the grout is still wet. Be sure to wipe away combined adhesive and grout or waterproof grout quickly – these are hard to clean off the tile surface once set.

4 To give the tiling a neat professional finish, run a thin piece of dowelling over each grout line. Or use the cap of a ball-point pen, the blunt end of a pencil or a lolly stick. Wipe surplus off the surface of the tiles as you go.

5 Leave the grout to dry, then polish the dusty film off the surface of the tiles using a clean, dry cloth.

Drilling holes through tiles

Many bathroom and kitchen accessories, like soap racks or towel rails, must be screwed to the wall – in which case you may have to drill holes through ceramic tiles.

It's a good idea to make fixings in tiled walls by drilling into grout lines wherever possible, but sometimes drilling through the glaze is unavoidable. Drilling through tiles creates a lot of fine dust, which may stain nearby grouting. To catch the dust, make a simple cardboard tray and stick it to the wall with masking tape or get someone to hold a vacuum-cleaner nozzle near the drill tip as you drill the hole.

Tools *Drill; small masonry bit to make pilot hole and larger one to suit the screw, or sharp spear point bit; chinagraph pencil; screwdriver; possibly steel ruler.*

Materials *Masking tape; wall plugs; screws.*

1 Decide where you want to make the screw fixing and mark its position on the surface of the tile with a chinagraph pencil.

2 Stop the point of the masonry bit from skating over the smooth tile surface by sticking a piece of masking tape over the mark, which should show through it. Re-make the mark on the surface of the tape. If you need to make more than one screw hole, use a strip of tape to cover both hole positions and mark them on the tape.

3 Make a pilot hole with the small masonry bit. Press the tip firmly against the mark on the tape. Check the drill isn't on hammer action, and start at a low speed. Drill slowly and carefully through the glazed surface of the tile. Stop drilling when the bit starts to penetrate the plaster. Using a small bit to do this minimises the risk of cracking the glaze. Repeat the process to drill any further holes.

4 Switch to the bit that matches the screw size you intend to use. Position its tip in the hole and drill slowly and carefully through the tile and the plaster and well into the masonry.

Alternatively You can buy a special ceramic tile bit with a sharp spear point. Its shape is designed to break through the glaze immediately. This minimises the risk of skidding across or cracking the tile. The drill bits are available in a range of sizes.

HELPFUL TIP

If you are putting a wall plug into a tiled wall, make the hole at least 3mm deeper than the length of the plug so that it can be pushed into the wall and beyond the tile. Otherwise, when you drive in the screw, the sideways pressure may crack the tile.

Laying mosaic tiles

Mosaic tiles come in sheets with a fabric mesh backing. They are a good DIY option, being much easier to fit around obstacles than full-size ceramic tiles.

Tools *Straightedge; spirit level; tape measure; pencil; notched adhesive spreader; wood batten; trimming knife; cutting board; tile-cutting pliers; grouting tools.*

Materials *Mosaic tiles; tile adhesive; grout.*

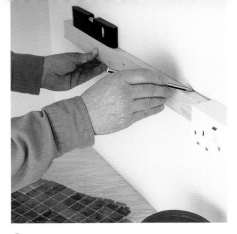

1 Use a batten and spirit level to mark out in pencil the area you want to tile. This simple splashback is the height of a sheet of tiles above the worktop.

2 Apply tile adhesive, holding the notched spreader at an angle of 45° to create ridges of an even depth.

5 Once you have cut out the section of tiles, check the fit. There will be gaps, but you can fill these later. Spread adhesive on the wall and put the cut sheet in place.

6 Lay all the whole and cut sheets until the area is covered. Then measure the small gaps left round any obstacles. These will need to be filled with individually cut tiles.

3 Put up the first sheet of tiles, lining it up with the guideline. Press it into place with your hand, then use a wood offcut to tamp the tiles level – especially those at the edges of the sheet.

4 When you reach an obstacle, such as a socket outlet, use a sharp trimming knife to cut out sections of whole mosaic tiles. Lay the sheet of tiles on a cutting board and run the blade along the gaps.

7 Use cutting pliers to cut single mosaics. First trim off a strip of tiles, then score a cutting line along the whole strip. Detach individual tiles and use the v-shaped jaws of the pliers to snap one tile at a time. Butter the back of each tile and fit into place.

8 Leave the adhesive to dry for 24 hours. Then grout the gaps between the tiles. Load a rubber-edged grout spreader with waterproof grout and draw it across the tiles. Clean surplus grout off the tile surfaces as you work. Before the grout sets, use a piece of slim dowel to neaten the grout lines (see page 120).

Painting tips for bathrooms and kitchens

Surface preparation, walls and ceilings

Before applying paint to walls or ceilings, check that the surface is sound, clean and dry. New plaster in particular must be completely dry.

General preparation Remove any loose or flaking paint; if necessary, wash the surface to remove dirt and grease. Any areas that have been affected by mould growth should be treated with a proprietary fungicidal wash.
Fill any cracks and holes with suitable filler and rub down smooth when dry.
Rub down or wash with sugar soap to remove any sheen, then dust with a damp lint-free cloth. Wear a dust mask if dry sanding so as to avoid inhaling dust.
Seal new, bare and porous surfaces. Bare plaster can be sealed with emulsion paint diluted with 20 per cent water, or with a proprietary plaster sealer. If decorating a newly plasterboarded wall (that has not been plastered), it is advisable to apply a coat of proprietary plaster sealer, as this type of surface is very absorbent.

Painting over wallcoverings Not all wallpapers are suitable for painting. Check first by painting an area of about 1m². If the paper bubbles and lifts, it will need to be stripped.
If painting lining paper, stir in about 10 per cent clean water to the paint.

Applying paint to walls and ceilings

The longer kitchen and bathroom paint is left to harden before being subjected to high humidity or condensation, the better its moisture resistance will be.

If walls are half tiled or kitchen units/bathroom fittings are already in position, it is worth spending time carefully protecting everything with dust sheets before you start painting. Use masking tape to stick dust sheets to the top edges of tiled walls.

Choosing the right paint

Walls and ceilings Specially formulated kitchen and bathroom paints are moisture resistant, washable and hardwearing. They will not peel away when exposed to a lot of steam. A silk or sheen finish is also easier to clean than a matt one. Despite its name, however, kitchen and bathroom paint will not withstand being soaked – do not use in a shower enclosure. Clean brushes with water and detergent.

Kitchen and bathroom paint is not suitable for use on radiators or hot water pipes.

Doors, skirtings and window frames
The best paint for woodwork is gloss paint. The glossier the paint, the tougher and more durable the surface will be. Unless it is labelled 'one-coat' or similar, all gloss paint should be applied over an undercoat, or, in the case of new bare wood, a primer and an undercoat.
Solvent-based gloss paints are the most hardwearing and the best choice in a hardworking kitchen. They are slow to dry and smell strongly during application. Be sure to open windows and doors while painting. Clean brushes in white spirit.
Water-based gloss is slightly less hardwearing. It dries quickly and has little odour. Brushes can be cleaned in water and detergent.

Radiators and pipes Gloss paint is suitable for use on pipes and radiators. It needs no undercoat when applied to copper pipework. Paint labelled 'radiator enamel' will not lose its whiteness through repeated heating and cooling.

1 Paint the ceiling first so as to avoid spoiling the walls with spatters. The best tool for painting the ceiling is a roller. Make sure you can safely reach the area you are decorating. Paint in strips starting near the window. Cut in the edges as you work.

2 Once the ceiling has been painted and is dry, you can paint the walls. You may need to apply only one coat, but if you are covering a contrasting colour, you will probably need to use two. Allow at least five hours between coats. In cold weather or an unheated room, leave more time for the first coat to dry fully.

3 Starting at the top of the wall, apply the paint in all directions working horizontally across the surface and moving down when one band is complete.

4 Lay off the paint with light brush strokes and a fairly dry brush, working in a criss-cross pattern. Lift the paint finally on upward strokes.

Applying paint to radiators and copper pipes

Make sure that all metalwork is clean and free from grease before painting. Wash previously painted pipes and radiators with a sugar soap solution, rinse and dry. Never paint a hot radiator – let it cool completely. Be careful not to paint over control valves; they must be free to turn.

1 Clean copper pipes with fine wire wool.

2 Apply gloss paint direct with a 25mm or 50mm brush. There is no need for primer. Undercoat is only needed on radiators and pipes if there is to be a colour change. Keep the coat as thin as possible so as to avoid runs.

A,B,C

airlocks 32
appliances
      freestanding 4, 10, 43, 50, 72-73
      integrated 48, 50
basins 82
      countertop basin 98-99
      replacing 96-97
bathroom 82-109
      electrical work 21, 106-9
      heating options 18-19
      internal, windowless bathroom 89
      lighting 82-83, 88-89
      order of work 95
      painting 123-4
      planning 82-83, 95
      plumbing 90-105
      storage 87
      styles 84-85
baths
      cast-iron 100-1
      enamel 100
      installing 101
      plastic 100
      renovating and repairing 100
      shower baths 83
      standard sizes 82
      taps, changing 100
      tiling around 113
bidets 83, 96-97
Building Regulations 20
cable routes
      bathrooms 21
      kitchens 43, 52-53, 72
carousels and corner units 46-47
ceramic tiles, removing 51
cold water cistern 12, 14, 32
      draining 23
      raising 91
cold water supply 10-11
combination (combi) boilers 12, 92
consumer unit 73
cooker
      fitted 48
      freestanding 48
      see also electric cooker
cooker hoods 48
Corian 45

D,E,F

decoration
      surface preparation 112
      see also painting; tiling
dishwasher, plumbing in 70-71
drainage 15
      re-routing 95, 98
      single stack system 15, 99
      two pipe system 15, 99

drawer shelves 46
drinking water 11
dry (airing) cupboard 87
electric cooker
      circuit 22, 74-75
      control unit 72, 74
      free-standing 72-73, 74
      separate oven and hob 75
      wiring in 72-73
electrical circuits
      isolating 22
      lighting circuit 16
      ring main circuit 16
      single-appliance circuit 17, 22, 74-5
electrical system 16-17
electrical work
      bathrooms 21, 106-9
      cable core colours 20
      earthing 106
      kitchens 43, 52-53, 72-79
      professional 20
      turning off the power 22
      Wiring Regulations 20, 21
extractor fans 43, 50, 83, 89
fire safety 77
flooring
      ceramic tiles, removing 51
      kitchen 43, 51
      quarry tiles 51
      taking up old flooring 51
fused connection unit (FCU) 106, 107-8

G,H,I,J

gas supply 50
heating
      plinth heaters 18, 48
      underfloor heating 18-19, 89
      see also radiators
hobs 48, 75
hot water cylinder 12, 13, 14
hot water supply 12-13
      direct systems 12-13
      indirect systems 12, 14
      instantaneous systems 12
      unvented (sealed) systems 12
immersion heater 12, 13
imperial/metric measurements 66, 98
joints
      pipework 66-67
      waste pipes 65, 68
      WC pan joints 103
      woodwork 58

K,L,M

kitchen 42-79
      appliances and fittings 48-49, 50
      electrical work 43, 52-53, 72-79

heating options 18-19
layout 42-43, 50
order of work 50
painting 123-4
plumbing 53, 65-71
styles 44-45
working triangle 42-43
see also kitchen units
kitchen units 54-60
assembling 54
base units 55, 56
cornice, pelmet and plinths 57-59
door and drawer fronts 44
doors, hanging 59
fixing to stud partition walls 55
fixings and brackets 54, 57
flat-pack units 54, 57
freestanding 44
handles 45, 60
hinges, soft-closing 59
installing 55-57
legs, adjustable 55
storage solutions 46-47
under-cupboard lighting 43, 49, 78-79
wall units 56-57
worktops 43, 45, 60-64
ladder radiators 108
larder, pull-out 46
laundry bin 87
light switches
bathrooms 21
pull-cord switch 21
pull-cord switch, repairing 38-39
lighting
bathroom 21, 82-83, 88-89
directional spot lights 88
kitchen 43, 50, 76-79
recessed spotlights 76-77, 88
showers 88
sunlight pipes 89
under-cupboard lighting 43, 49, 78-79
lighting circuit 16
lighting pelmets 58
macerator units 95
medicine cabinets 82, 87
mirrors 88
mosaic tiles 121-2
mounting box 53

P,R,S,T

painting 123-4
pipes
airlocks 32
bending copper piping 53
blockages 32-33
communication pipe 10
joining 66-67
painting 123, 124
service pipe 10
see also waste pipes

plaster 112
plasterboard 112
plate drawers 46
plinth heaters 18, 48
plumbing
bathroom 90-105
kitchens 53, 65-71
pumps 91
radiators
ladder radiators 108
painting 123, 124
thermostatic radiator valves 18
towel rail radiators 18, 106
rising main 10, 14
shaver sockets 82, 106
fitting 109
shower baths 83
shower heads
descaling 38
spray roses 93
shower screens 83
shower-diverters 31
showers
bath tap attachments 86
flow rate 85
installation 105
instantaneous shower 90, 91, 92
lighting 88
mixer shower 90, 91, 92, 93, 94
power shower 92
pumps 91
shower trays 86, 93, 105
standard sizes 82
thermostatic control 85, 90, 91, 93
tower units 93
walk-in showers 83, 85, 86, 105
water pressure 90, 91
sink
blocked 32-33
inset sink 62-63
socket outlets 16, 50
connecting appliances to 106, 107
soil pipes 95
soil stack 15
splashbacks 61
tiling 113
stoptaps 10, 11, 23
jammed 23
storage
bathroom 87
kitchen 46-47
stud finder 76
stud walls, fixing to 55, 95
sunlight pipes 89
taps 26-31
airlocks 32
bathrooms 94, 100
ceramic disc tap 26
ceramic discs, cleaning/replacing 28-29
dripping 27-29
hard-water damage 28
high-neck taps 64
kitchens 49, 64

leaking 29-31
mixer taps 31, 32, 49, 64, 94
non-rising spindle 26
O-rings, renewing 30-31
pillar taps 94
rising spindle 26
self-cutting taps 71
shower-diverters 31
tap conversion kit 28, 96
valve seating, repairing 28
see also stoptaps
tiling
around a bath 113
around corners 118-19
around a window 117
ceramic tiles, removing 51
cutting tiles to fit 116-17
drilling holes through 121
grout and sealant 112, 120
half-tiling a wall 113-14
mosaic tiles 121-2
over tiles 112
splashbacks 113
tile layout 112-13
a wall 115-16
window recess 119
worktops 112
tiling gauge 114
towel rail radiators 18, 106
towel rails, heated 18, 87, 106
connecting 109
toy storage 87
traps 15
anti-siphon bottle trap 69
bath traps 94
fitting 69
kitchen traps 69
standard bottle trap 94
tubular trap 69
washing-machine trap 69

V,W

valves
drain valve 23
gatevalve 23
service valves 22, 23
ventilation see extractor fans
washing machine
plumbing in 70-71
trap 69
waste, kitchen 47
waste pipes 15, 65, 92
fitting 68
joints 65, 68
linking into 99
self-cutting waste pipe 71
waste water 15
water mains 10
water meter 10
water pressure 11
water softeners and purifiers 11
water supply
cold water supply 10-11
hot water supply 12-13
turning off 22-23
water tanks 12, 14
WCs
ballvalve adjustment 34
close-coupled WC 36, 103, 104
faulty cistern 34-35
flap valve, renewing 35-36
moving 95
pan joints 103
push-button cistern 37
replacing 102-4
seat, replacing 37
siting 83
standard siphon 35
standard sizes 82
two-part syphon 36
wetrooms 84, 85, 92
Wiring Regulations 21
worktops 43, 45, 60-64
acrylic blends 45
cutting to fit 60-61
edging strip 64
fixing and finishing 63-64
granite 45
hardwood 45
inset sink 62-63
laminate 45, 60-1
splashbacks 61
stainless steel 45
tiling 112
upstands 61
worktop rail 47

INDEX

Acknowledgments

All images in this book are copyright of the Reader's Digest Association Limited, with the exception of those in the following list.

The position of photographs and illustrations on each page is indicated by letters after the page number:
T = Top; **B** = Bottom; **L** = Left; **R** = Right; **C** = Centre

The majority of images in this book are © Reader's Digest and were previously published in Reader's Digest *DIY Manual*, *1001 DIY Hints & Tips* and Reader's Digest *First-time Homeowner's DIY Manual.*

Front Cover © Reader's Digest, **TR** 'Academy' by Ideal Standard, **CL** 'Kyomi' by Ideal Standard. **Back Cover** © Reader's Digest **18 BL** Myson Radiators **38 BR, 39** GE Fabbri Limited **44** Tim Wood Tel: 07041380030 **45 T** Red Cover/Mark Bolton **CL** Red Cover/Johnny Bouchier **BL** Red Cover/Mark Bolton **45 BR** Red Cover/Winfried Heinze **46 T** Red Cover/ Simon McBride **CR** Eggersman Kitchens www.eggersmann.co.uk **BL** Red Cover/Huntley Hedworth **47 T** Eggersman Kitchens www.eggersmann.co.uk **B** Nolte Kitchens UK www.noltekitchens.co.uk/ **48 T** Elizabeth Whiting & Associates/Neil Davis **B** Getty Images Ltd/Johnny Bouchier **49 T** Franke UK www.franke.co.uk **C** Elizabeth Whiting & Associates/Neil Davis **B** © Wildscape / Alamy Images **64 TR** www.bathstore.com 'XT' washbasin mixer **BR** 'Academy' by Ideal Standard **82-83** © Reader's Digest/HL Studios **84** Red Cover/Winfried Heinze **85 T** Red Cover/Ed Reeve **B** Bathrooms International www.bathroomsint.com **86 B** Corbis/William Geddes/Beateworks **T** Getty Images Ltd/Winfried Heinze **87 L** Radiating Style www.radiatingstyle.com **R** Homestyle Bathrooms www.homestyle-bathrooms.co.uk **88** Red Cover/James Silverman **89 T** Red Cover/Henry Wilson **R** Monodraught www.sunpipe.co.uk **94 TL** 'Millenia QT' by Armitage Shanks **115** GE Fabbri Limited **118 TR & BR, 119, 122** GE Fabbri Limited

Reader's Digest Kitchen & Bathroom DIY Manual is based on material in *Reader's Digest DIY Manual*, published by The Reader's Digest Association Limited, London.

First Edition Copyright © 2007
The Reader's Digest Association Limited,
11 Westferry Circus, Canary Wharf,
London E14 4HE
www.readersdigest.co.uk

Origination Colour Systems Limited, London
Printed and bound in China by CT Printing

The contents of this book are believed to be accurate at the time of printing. However the publisher accepts no responsibility or liability for any work carried out in the absence of professional advice.

We are committed to both the quality of our products and the service we provide to our customers. We value your comments, so please feel free to contact us on 08705 113366, or via our website at www.readersdigest.co.uk

If you have any comments about the content of our books, email us at gbeditorial@readersdigest.co.uk

The Reader's Digest Association Limited would like to thank the following people and organisations for their help in the production of this book: Roger Anstee, John Bowsher, Peter Camacho, Sue and Lawrence Chater, Sean Lawes and John Lister. Kitchen fitting photography taken with the help of *Kitchens by Design*, Pickwick Limited, 2 Abacus House, Newlands Road, Corsham, Wiltshire SN13 0BH. 01249 701177 www.pickwicklimited.com

Editor Alison Candlin
Art Editor Julie Bennett
Assistant Editor Helen Spence
Editorial Consultant Mike Lawrence
Additional photography Gary Ombler
Proofreader Ron Pankhurst
Indexer Marie Lorimer

Reader's Digest General Books
Editorial Director Julian Browne
Art Director Nick Clark
Managing Editor Alastair Holmes
Head of Book Development Sarah Bloxham
Picture Resource Manager Sarah Stewart-Richardson
Pre-press Account Manager Sandra Fuller
Senior Production Controller Deborah Trott
Product Production Manager Claudette Bramble

ISBN: 978 0 276 44202 5
BOOK CODE: 400-612 UP0000-1
ORACLE CODE: 250010679H.00.24